TOUCHDOWN

Learning How to Score Curiosity,

Joy and Freedom in Adulthood

by

KATHERINE EASTVOLD

–

To my Father, who asked me to write this.
To Dr. John Omaha who made it possible.
To my husband Nick. I love you.

CONTENTS

Whoever is winning at the moment
will always seem to be invincible.
George Orwell

1 GAME ON

Life is a game of football. People will tell you it's not. They will tell you to simply "envision" the ball crossing the goal line and your body will get you there, automatically, as if your mental, physical and emotional states can all become aligned, in sync and extremely powerful by this one simple act of focus.

Too many make it sound easy, painting a picture of you floating over the ugliness, craziness and chaos that is life and crossing over that goal post and landing, unscathed, uninjured and perfectly peaceful, on the other side of those large looming posts... happy, content and in a state of "win."

Yeah. It's not like that, is it? While our eyes are closed, focusing on that golden apple of a goal post down the field, a linebacker tackles us. What the? Then a bunch of other big guns jump on top of him. We are so shocked and startled that you.... yup, you guessed it... drop the ball.

Ah. It's such a nice picture, that peaceful floatation device of a dream, isn't it? It takes no prisoners. No war. No violence. No conflict. No devices. It only requires us to keep an eye on what we want, not what we can't have, what's sneaking up on us, coming at us and most definitely not on the very real road blocks that are uniquely designed for each of us.

(You do know we have designer road blocks, right? One of a kind, high end, extremely effective road blocks for each of us. For free too! Prada did a really great job on them.)

But while the programs, meditations and techniques all train you in ways to rise above it all and, well, skip the crap, so to speak, we still seem to have a really difficult time actually doing this without disconnecting all ties to the relationships and world around us.

It's really hard to stay "above" it all for very long. We leave our loved ones behind, thinking we have the answers and they don't yet. We become so focused on ourselves that we simply lose empathy or compassion for others.

I don't understand the whole "being in the now" notion. It sounds still, stiff and rather alien. I rarely meet people who are both dedicated to their "pictures" of what they want and are also full of joy, freedom and curiosity. In other words, I haven't met a lot of people who've either danced on the other side of that goal line, making a major touchdown, or who are making a run for it, free and clear of any other opposing team members - all because of their ability to float. Or stay still. Or be "in" any certain kind of state of "being."

Wait. Strike that. I haven't met *any*.

The truth is that we are all down there on that field. And it's impossible to win the game without skills. Life skills. We have to have a great offense and we have to have a great defense. Period.

It's not pretty. It can get dirty. If we don't prepare, don't see the play, get caught unawares too often, we move farther and farther away down the field from success and our end zone. It's harder and harder to get that ball back down the field for a touchdown.

But we can. There's always a way. Sometimes it's luck. Most of the time it's skill. And luckily our four quarters are a lot longer than 15 minutes, though we really don't have a halftime, as much and as dearly as we may desire one.

Sometimes I think the New Age philosophies trick us into thinking we can win the game during the halftime show, when we are alone and no one is looking. I'm okay with that. I don't agree with it, I wouldn't necessarily ever promote it, but I will always let others make their own decisions for themselves. Go where you please.

I'm here for the ones who *don't* feel it connects the dots for them. I'm here for the ones who know life is down there on a field - who know it's a game - who know it's a challenge - and are still willing to face it, willing to learn it and ready to go out there and *win* it!

I've had a lot of training in this game. *A lot.*

I know how to protect the ball when I'm tripped, knocked or tackled. I've learned the different strategies of my opposing team. I've studied my "designer" road blocks. I've gotten to know their names, their widths, heights and weights. Oh and I've trained, oh how I've ever trained! Strengthened my knees, my legs, my reflexes and my back. I can dodge left, I can dodge right and I can spin with speed and agility around every person and play.

I've gotten to know my teammates. I've picked them carefully, because unlike so many people tell you, you *can* pick your own teammates. I know them well. I work with them well. Together we are powerful. Together we are a great team. Together, we're able to win.

Life is war. And you know it when you see it, don't you? They wear it clear as day. Whether, at the end of the line, someone has won the game... or not.

I fully intend on winning it. Are you? Then let's get to it. Hands together... (insert some inspiring chant. One that gets you jumpy and pumped...) aaaaaaand - BREAK! It's time to hit the field.

Let's go!

2 THE STADIUM
A New Kind of Stage

Each of our lives is built just like a stadium is. It's uncanny. We all have a playing field, we all have onlookers and we all have coaches, cheerleaders, etc. And, just like the football stadiums that grace our nation, each one of ours is different. Unique. Built perfectly for our teams.

Your stadium is amazing, majestic and tailored in many ways to you. So is mine. But in the essentials we are the same. And it's the essentials I'm going to lay out for you right now. These are the building blocks upon which our lives are built. Know how to utilize each section wisely and your opposition will find themselves faced with quite the opponent.

First there's your playing field. It's just as large, dramatic and looming as the ones you see in high definition during the Super Bowl. That long, wide stretch of green grass and turf is the stage upon which your life is lived. Played. Determined.

- Playing the Field -

Every moment you're on that field you want the ball to be in your hands, not the others.' You want to move it towards your goal line, not away from it. And because you will always have an opposing team, you will always need to be ready for them.

In order to win though, you need to be more than just ready. Especially when the stakes are as high as they are - this is your life. You don't want to be some set of stats and the end of your game.

Even the worst teams in history have stats. That's not what you're here for.

You need special training to win on that playing field. It can be energizing, lifting and exciting when you're finally winning and playing the game right. But to get there you need to have the right team, the right coaching, the best support system and the most incredible playbook ever. Which you are about to receive.

And once you succeed, you can start aiming for the end zone without fear. Oh yes, our fields have end zones too. And the goal posts. The goal lines. The touchdowns. Oh! The glorious touchdowns! How much more powerful are the touchdowns in *our* stadiums!

Touchdowns are at the heart of this book. There are many different kinds, but all of them are important to make. They don't just affect us, but the world around us. It affects our future and it even affects how we view our future. We are built for touchdowns. We are built to win.

When we don't, our bodies know it. The stadium knows it. The atmosphere grows dim. It's hard to come back from a losing streak. But then again, it's hard to stop winning when you are on a winning streak too. So it's time to start winning, asap. And the way we do that is to start making the kind of touchdowns with the greatest impact first.

So many out there tell us to start at the top of the heap that is our lives and slowly dig our way down to the bottom, where the real troubles lay. Or to look at it another way, some people want to trim the tree that is our life - trim it back, further and further until finally you can see the trunk.

And then, once the trunk is exposed, you can trim your way right down to the roots. And once you're finally down to the roots - Oh! - Shocking! - The roots are bad. We'll have to dig them out and replant a new tree. No kidding.

I say we start at the bottom and the rest will follow. I say we heal the roots first and - Hey - The tree will get better! That's just my approach. Much quicker. Deeper- less easy- but wonderfully warm, yet hopeful, with just a touch of giggle in there.

These are the touchdowns we need to make first. These are the vital goals that, once we hit the scoreboard with them, will turn your game around. Shake up your stadium a bit. Wake everyone up.

It's time to get back to winning again. And how.

- Touchdowns -

Not all touchdowns are equal in our stadiums. The most important ones are built upon the ones that came before them. They require strength that only previous touchdowns can provide. It's the nature of growing. A simple example is our children. They don't just stand up and walk after being held for so long. No, there's a long process of building - taking things step, by step, by step.

I loved seeing this first hand for the first time in my oldest nephew. I remember watching him learn to turn himself over onto his tummy. It took so much effort at first, for him to simply roll from his back to his front.

You know the rest - then came propping himself up on his own. Then came the crawling... then the standing and then, oh! There he goes! Walking quickly but wobbly to his dad. It's a marvelous process to watch, if ever you have the luxury of time, to sit and see them test themselves, watch them move, learning how to use their own bodies.

Each step, each skill, is required for the next and more advanced type of movement.

None of it had to do with attitude though. It wasn't my nephew's attitude that gave him the desire to roll over. I know a child's curiosity has a lot to do with it, I'm sure, but it was a natural progression of growing.

We are like that. There's something in us that just wants to grow. To move forward. To build ourselves.

Which is my point about starting with the vital touchdowns first. We could start at the top and make easy touchdowns first, building our team's morale and confidence. But I promise you, there are a whole lot of touchdowns to score before you reach all the way down to the vital ones, and by then, you will be quite tired.

Scoring *any* kind of touchdown without a clean, strong and healthy team will take you years... decades even. I can't imagine you'd be in the best mood by then. But let's say you went ahead and made the vital touchdown somehow... how much time, money or community do you have left to enjoy the fruit of it?

Investing in your stadium, your field and your team will become easier and easier as you go. You'll see the fruits immediately. The coming touchdowns in this book will unravel a world of possible touchdowns for you that never would have existed otherwise. But they need so much more than a good attitude to attain. Don't cheat yourself out of an amazing game by thinking you have to "be ready" to get on that field without fear, without doubt or without pain.

I've been there. I've even made a number of touchdowns with nothing more than a bad mood. Not all of them, but there were definitely some of them. They just aren't easy ones to make, these foundational and/or vital touchdowns. But I know what needs to be done to make the touchdown that is good for me in the long run. I totally pout as I'm running down that field with the ball, but watch me - I do the work. I make the choice. I make the touchdown.

Not because I feel like it, but because I've learned too well what happens if I don't make it.

I look down that road (field) in front of me and see two futures - the one with the touchdown and the one without. And I get it. I see it. The two roads. The two futures. And I make a choice. I jam myself down that field, plow through my triggers and my pitfalls, and slam the ball down in the end zone.

I may not be smiling, but I made the right choice. The hard choice. Sometimes there isn't a crowd to cheer on those touchdowns. They never saw it made, because I played it when they weren't in the stadium. I played it alone.

Sometimes they do see it and they see the cost and they just stare. On those days and on those touchdowns the cheerleaders don't jump up in the air and the crowd doesn't cheer your name. They just watch. They don't understand the play. Those kinds of plays are rarely seen anymore. They are from a different time, a different age... long, long past. But you do. You weighed and measured and took it to the end zone. And that's what matters.

No, not all touchdowns are alike. But they are all, *all* necessary in order to win the game.

- Out of Bounds -

It's time to shake some hands with those who are on your sidelines. You'll find that your coaches and assistant coaches are there, as well as your cheerleaders, etc. They are just as instrumental to you and your game, if not more, as in football. But be ready - this support team can be a whole lot more temperamental then your average sideliners, which is hard to do, I know, but be on your guard and be ready to take a good look at them with me later on anyhow.

Behind the sidelines, just as in most stadiums, there are the stands. Your stands are full of all kinds of people. Your family, friends, co-workers, loved ones and even the people you walk by everyday. They all watch the game of your life being played out, to one varying degree or another, from up close to far away. There are a lot of places to sit in stadiums, and sometimes you can't even see them all from down on the field, but there they are.

You are also a visitor in the stadiums of the people you are close to too. Time spent in each other's stands can make huge differences in each of your games when done the right way. The more closely you watch each other's games the healthier your relationship tends to be, generally speaking. Good relationships are made up of people who care about the games we are playing against our opposition. They care about how we're doing out there. Who doesn't love a good play-by-play every once in a while, right?

Sometimes, though, we're in other people's stadiums and we don't even know it. Being aware of who influences you and what games you watch really can affect your own game. It's amazing how much we absorb every day. It's good to be making those choices yourself, instead of wandering into somebody's stadium without even knowing it - whether you're sitting in the nosebleed section or not.

Your stadium has a lot of others things too, including locker rooms and the ever elusive opposing team. We will get to them - but only when we're ready with enough information to recognize them when we see them. So let's start with the very first touchdown every winning team has to make: successful tryouts!

3 YOUR TEAM
The Most Important Cut Ever

To win the game of your life, to score a touchdown, *any* touchdown, you have to have the right team. This sounds obvious. The roster of a team is the fodder of every news channel on every station in every city. It's hard to escape the news coverage of who is playing for whom and which player is being dropped from which team. It's everywhere, and for a good reason.

That roster is everything. There are millions upon millions of dollars riding on every name they've signed. The only people telling you your roster doesn't matter are the people who are rooting for the other team. Period.

And how do we know a roster is good? Their scoreboards. The team's success. The team's statistics. If a team is winning all the time, building upon their success, gaining recognition and playing well together, we call them a great team. It's not because we like them, think they are entertaining or cute. It's the scores that count.

This is why coaches aren't sentimental. They have make cuts with the scoreboard in mind. It's their job. It's what they do best. They keep the entire team's health, well-being and success in the forefront of their minds at all times.

No one is cut from a team based on their good looks, charm or personality. They are cut because they hold their team back on the field. It has nothing to do with love and everything to do with survival.

I want you to remember that. When it comes to your team, you are going to have to adopt the same principles. We have to keep our eye on the scoreboard when we pick our teammates. Compromise and you lose. There's no in between.

Just as in football, you are either winning a game or losing it. And just as winning the game of life has much more potential than winning a game of football, losing in life is much more costly too. Keeping your roster trim and fit in order to win is most definitely worth it. But it isn't always easy either.

Keeping all of this in mind, let's go for it. Let's get you the best roster possible. You deserve it. You were built for it. We all were. We were all designed with winning in mind. We were all given what it takes. But something broke along the way. It's not as easy now, no, but it's most definitely possible.

Who is your stadium built for? Your team. Who did everyone come to see play? Your team. Who does your opposing team want to trounce because you are valuable? Your team.

You need to get the roster right. You *must* get the roster right.

Prepare to cut some of your teammates. Every team has cuts in the beginning. They all have tryouts and they all make cuts. Every single year. They know just how easy it is to go wrong. They know just how important it is to get it right.

Every team has cuts. Or I should say every *winning* team has cuts. Chin up. You can do it. Let's start with a roll call first.

- Tryouts -

It is common sense to take a method and try it.
If it fails, admit it frankly and try another.
But above all, try something.
Franklin D. Roosevelt

This roll call is actually going to require a paper and pen. There aren't any other exercises in this book, but this one's a pretty important one all the same. You can do this on your phone or tablet too, but I have to be straight with you - studies and research tell us that writing with pen and paper make dramatic changes to the brain and always for the better. This exercise is no exception.

So let's begin. Go ahead and title your paper "My Team" and then write in the date in the top right hand corner. This piece of paper might be very special to you one day.

Now go ahead and close your eyes for a second. Imagine you are on the playing field of your stadium. Look up and around you.

Look at all the stands in every direction. Now, look down the field and see your opposition.

They are a group of all shapes and sizes, all of whom scare, intimidate or overwhelm you on some level. Think about all the roadblocks they throw your way, the hang-ups, the bullies, the bills and the tricks or games people play on or around you.

Now look at your side of the field. See the grass and the white lines against it. Who is standing next to you? Who are the faces of your team? Who's making plays, interceptions and passes alongside you? Start running towards your opposition... does anyone else appear on your field with you? Who?

Now go for it. Write down everyone.

Write down the names of those who play next to you everyday. Who helps you survive your life today? Your lifestyle? The world around you? Go ahead and write down anyone you can think of. If you're not sure, then write their names down too. Trust your instincts on this exercise. If their names are popping into your head or leaning against your heart, include their names on your team roster.

Now, try to list the names of those who have been on your team in the past, or who come on your team here and there throughout the years. I know life changes. There are hard times, good times and all the times in-between. In order to survive all the variations we often turn to a variety of different helpers.

This includes names of things other than people. Remember that steroids and other supporting "aids" are a huge part of the sporting industry. There is a reason for this. Players try things once, then try them again and then they simply can't play without them. It happens all the time. So they turn to a myriad of other aids to survive.

We do the very same thing. It's so easy to get caught up in, especially when we live in a culture where it's considered okay. So many people live in an addictive system and don't even know it. They think drinking everyday is okay. They think treating their pets like people are normal things to do. There are all kinds of things we turn to and suddenly they become a vital part of our day.

So they end up as part of our teams without us even realizing it. How well could you survive your day without those things? List them just in case. This is not about whether you have a problem or not. This is simply taking inventory of who your teammates are:

people, person or thing.

Some people use fashion, some people use video games and many, many others use pornography. That's right - not all of our team members are shiny happy people, are they? We have a lot of things on that field for us that can be tough, be ugly or be angry when we feel like we can't be.

Which brings us to the people you *don't* want on your team, but are on there anyway. Who pushes their way onto your field? Who begs to be on your team? Who are you hesitant to call, but you call anyway? Write down all the pushy people or insistent helpers who need, want and insist to be on your team right there on your roster. Just because you don't want them there, doesn't mean they aren't playing for you.

Write them all down. This is important. The men, the women or the parents you hide behind in certain situations all qualify as teammates of yours. If there is anyone out there taking hits for you - like bills, car payments, house payments, workloads, school loans... on and on and on - these are all tactics used in our game. List their names on there too.

For the purpose of this assignment, be sure to go way back in time too. Go allllll the way back - right back to your very first day as an adult. 18 is a good place to start. Or graduation from high school. Graduation from college is pushing it.

That's because college is precisely designed to let you use and develop your adult skills. If you are enrolled in college but are living at home, going to school and not really holding down a job, then you're pretty much still in high school. If you're still living at home *after* college, even when you have a job, then you will probably have a lot of names on that team roster of yours.

But I have to say, if that's the case, adulthood might not be something you're interested in. It might not be something your parents are interested in either. Not all parents can handle having their kids out of the house anymore. They need them there to feel purposeful and fulfilled.

As such, there is a growing movement in the US where parents are increasingly allowing their educated kids to live at home because the kids say it's "too expensive" out there. But these "kids" have Armani jeans and a beamer. Uh huh. That's not much different than a life that's Christmas Day. Those kinds of high end labels and nice cars used to be a sign of success for older adults who have succeeded in life and have worked hard.

Now they are almost always worn and driven instead by young twenty-somethings who are spending other people's money. Entire resorts and casinos in Las Vegas have been renovated to cater to the young crowd who are using everyone's money but their own. The other high end resorts in Vegas are being designed for the foreign markets, not the rest of the US.

Vegas is such a fabulous little tear in the time continuum. What happens there reflects so many of the shifts in our cultures. It's like seeing the future, loud and clear. I never go there to gamble. I go there to interview the staff, the clientele and study the shifts in the landscapes of every level of Vegas, from the demographics at each hotel to the types of goods being advertised and sold there.

It's been a while since I've seen a majority of old money there. But the flood of young money just keeps flowing. At the tables, on the strip, in the clubs. Fascinating. But what happens when their parent's or grandparent's retirement and savings accounts are empty? I'm waiting for the answer to appear. I have a feeling it will be coming soon.

Anyhow, if you are in that crowd, then yes, you'll need to write down a few big money names on your team's roster.

If you're stuck or having trouble remembering some of your teammates, then here are some other common areas of life when we ask others to step in and fight for us. Consider anniversaries, special milestones or the times we face loss, hardship, ugliness and/or despair. Who is on your field playing with you then?

Consider too those times when you are in transition. When life is changing, when you are moving or when work is floundering - who do you need on your field with you? Be thorough, be honest, and again, if you can't decide, list their names. You're thinking of them for a reason.

This will change you as you write. You will learn about yourself and your relationships. It's amazing how the physical act of writing works in us. As I said, pen and paper tends to rule over keyboards or voice recordings when it comes to these kinds of things.

It does amazing things for your mental, emotional and physical health. So do yourself a favor and take the time to sit. Sit down. And scrawl out the list of your teammates, even if it means putting me and my book down and taking a break to finish your team roster before coming back.

Just come back. Please! We're about to get *very* yummy.

———

Are you back? Good. Great! I understand if you need some time to rest. You're digging into the foundation of your life here. It's bringing up a lot of memories, a lot of truth and *a lot* of feelings. If there were ever a time to take a hot bath or go for a massage, this would be it.

When you're all settled, rested and ready to dig in again, we'll get started. The next part, the cut, is going to be your very first big touchdown. I promise. Touchdowns are rather big milestones these days, so it will be exciting and, as team cuts usually are, unexpected. Still, cuts are never easy. Coaches never look forward to reading them aloud. But I think you're ready. More than ready!

So let's talk about your first hard decision of the book.

- The Cut -

First and foremost, you must remember that when a head coach cuts his team, he isn't cutting anyone out of the stadium. Remember this. Everyone who tries out for a team is always welcome to the games themselves. They can watch, assist, cheer and more, even if they aren't on the field playing the game.

It's the same for us and our own team rosters. You are not about to cut any of the names you've listed on there out of your life. Of course you always can if you want to. You may have figured that out while writing up your team's roster. But this cut we're discussing is regarding your team only. It only defines who is allowed to play for your team on your playing field. Only.

Now, I'm about to give you the secret to having a *winning* roster. I'm going to do more than that, actually. I'm going to help you not only develop your winning roster, but strengthen it, arm it and give you the insider info that will enable your team to slam through and break the incredibly large wall that is your opposing team. Yes. I am.

The thing is, all of this training will not work unless you actually follow through with the cut. A winning roster is the very first piece to the puzzle. It's a must. Add even one cut player back on to the list, and the whole thing is compromised. Think about any and all other team sports.

Who in the world would send their team out onto the field of a huge stadium of any kind, with the handicap of an "off" player? No one. It would change the whole team. That's the joy and the beast of the team sports. Every single player counts. The same goes for you. There can be no fudging on this issue.

So. Here we are. Are you ready for it? Who made the cut? I'll tell you.

In order to make *any* kind of touchdown, a field goal, a flying leap into your end zone, with bombs bursting in air while the crowds go wild...

well...

None of the people on your list can be on your team.
None of them.
Not the mothers, the brothers, the sisters or the lovers... not one.
The only person on that field should be...

You.
Yes, *you.*
You. Yourself. Tu. Toi. Your person. Your body.
You.

I know. It's scandalous. I totally agree with you. I thought the same things too.

And I am so sorry. I know that's not what you expected to hear, or that it's even easy to hear, especially considering the list I just asked you to take the time to write. Keep that list handy though! It's going to be a powerful tool in the future.

But still, this is the cold, hard, amazing and tantalizing truth; *you* are your win roster. And nobody else.

I know it's a shock. But you can do it. I can do it. We can do it. Why? How do I know? Because it's been done before.

There were days when such news as this, that the only way you can conquer life is to lift it and break it with your own hands, and your own hands alone, would not have been so surprising. It would have been an assumption. Nearly every piece of land on this planet has seen the generations before us... and every piece of land knows we could not match them in battle.

We, especially the western society, are no longer used to

knowing our own power. It's not just because we no longer work with our hands - which is part of it, of course, yes - but it is not all of it. That's only half of it. Look at those who still mold the earth beneath us, who farm the land or build our buildings - they would not fear such a thing as a winning roster with their own names on it. They've learned how much our bodies can handle - they can handle a great, great deal.

But the other half, the things that really terrify us the most of us about this "winning" team roster, is the emotional support we'll be losing. Either that, or the financial support. But those who came before us knew how to handle such things as well. They knew how to rest, how to mourn and how to grow up. We are their offspring, are we not? So why can't we?

Because society is fleeing from the idea of adulthood and pushing us more and more into a cartoon-ish world, where we are all still kids, silly and wild. You can see it everywhere, from music artists who wear masks and cartoon-like hair and makeup, to television shows where huge popping eyes and over-exuberant hand movements are everywhere.

There's little difference between the shows on Nickelodeon to the shows on prime time. In ad after ad, show after show, it's the kids who are the smart ones and it's the adult's who need to learn from them. And if kids aren't a part of the program, then there's and adult who is acting like a kid.

It's a brilliant marketing strategy.

Kids aren't responsible. Kids don't have to budget. Kids don't have to worry about money. Kids don't have to consider the consequences. Kids don't have to have to say "no" to fun. So the media markets and the global commerce systems fill us and infuse us with the idea that if we are adults in anyway, then we are *wrong*. Putting limits on ourselves is something "old," and spending money and acting childish is not only "young and hip," but *normal* - even smart!

No wonder we struggle with debt. No wonder adults wear teenage clothing. No wonder we're scared of taking on our opposing team by ourselves.

But if you think about it, it was not so long ago that we were highly functioning adults, excited to go out on our own. There was a time we sat at the kids table and looked longingly up... yearning for the day we could sit there and discuss adult things with adult voices. Even if it's the other way around now, it really doesn't have to be. Not for us.

I was watching an award winning show from the late 80's yesterday. My culture shock was incredible. It portrayed a couple's newly adult children facing some of the first waves of difficulty in their new adult lives.

And oh! How those kids were insistent upon being self-reliant! They were so excited to build their own future, their own home and their own jobs. I nearly fell out of my seat. My husband is an engineer and his firm employs about twenty young men and women who have degrees and make excellent pay. Only one has an apartment... and he's married.

The rest? At home.

Yet this show aired only 15 short years ago. Incredible. It's not impossible you guys. We can remember how to be adults again. We can learn how to be the only name on our roster. We are not the first, but we can be great again.

If you look even farther back in time, you will remember how great we once were. Men and women pioneered so many areas and so many nations. We have won wars. We have fought for freedom. Generations upon generations before us have faced great evils and won. On their own.

I get the feeling, sometimes, that we know our souls have been suppressed - that our greatness has been quieted. I see it in the young people sometimes - they are itching to be empowered instead of being taken care of. I see that some are starting to stand up, look over the status quo and consider the horizons of adventure.

Adventure. Adventure is the sign that tells you if you are your own team or not. Those who go up against their own opposing teams face so much more adventure than those of us who don't. Remember, living is to play the game. If you have others playing for you, then you are not living.

Living is very much like adventure. They go hand in hand. That's practically all you will face on that field. Facing any opposing team requires danger and excitement. There are good adventures and there are bad ones. There are good games and there are bad ones. Every game has its own story.

I remember when Nick and I first made the cuts required for our winning teams. Wow, it was hard. Not hard in the ways you might think. It was just so different. So new. So wonderful. We found out what we were made of. I love this quote:

> Do you want to know who you are? Don't ask. Act!
> Action will delineate and define you.
> *Thomas Jefferson*

Ex. Act. LY! I have lived this. My friends have now lived this. Oh, how much we are all discovering about ourselves and each other. Every time we see each other, there's another story to tell. Not one story has been boring. Ever.

Let me share you with you one of our first stories. Shortly after Nick and I made "the most important cut," we went on a road trip. A long one. We saw amazing things, took once in a lifetime pictures and almost never took a highway. We tried to say on the side roads as much as possible.

It was fantastic. We shared photos on Facebook. People loved watching us explore the world and it was a gleeful time. Until it wasn't. Something went very, very wrong. We ran into some bad characters. At first I was hesitant, then I was alarmed and then there was the terror.

I'd never felt terror like that before. Thank God we had the training that we did. In short, we were very much in tune with our instincts by that point and oh, how we listened to them. We went feral. Basic instinct. And we made it out alive.

The days that followed were some of the toughest of my life. We hadn't had anyone to hide behind. We didn't have anyone to step in for us. And we didn't have any parental voices telling us that we did a "good job" or that we were "very good" children.

Instead we just had friends who also had also made their cuts. The first said that I would write about it one day and help others. (Huh.) The second sent me the following quote:

"Adventure is not all pony-rides in May-sunshine."

It was from Tolkein's *The Hobbit*, if you can believe it. And the moment I read it I thought of the dragon and the spiders and of the infamous Gollum. And I felt like a fool.

How could I not have seen it? How could I possibly complain? I love adventure movies. I love adventure novels. I thought I loved adventure. I told everyone that I loved adventure. And yet here I was, shocked that I came across a dragon.

I've faced many a dragon since then. Shoot. I think I've faced much worse. By the time they made the Hobbit into a movie, Nick and I watched as if it were our own lives unfolding before us on the screen.

There's that scene in the beginning of the first movie, when Bilbo awoke after his company had gone... see it for yourself. The hole suddenly seemed vast and empty. There that lone candle sits, and its smoke slowly trails upwards.

Bilbo stands there next to it. Looking away. He had his chance at adventure. He didn't want it. He fought against it.

Then he couldn't stand it when it went away.

It is this that I offer you. A misty mountain. A dragon. A wilderness before you filled with things unknown. We love these tails of adventure and power - they stay with us for decade after decade for one single reason: they answer the call within us.

I invite you out into the extraordinary. I invite you to step into the unknown. I invite you to cut your teammates loose. I invite you to make the hardest cut ever.

- The Win Roster -

So let's start at the beginning again. Take your place on your playing field again. Close your eyes. Feel the list - your roster - surrounding you. It's time to pick them up and move them off your field. Take them each by hand if you have to, and move them off the field.

You can do it slowly, gently and calmly. You can do it forcefully. No matter what anyone says, you are in control of your field. No one can stand on it without your permission. And it's time to revoke all privileges to your field.

Make the most important cut, and release every single name into the stands. Keep them there. We will get to them later. For now, it's time to focus on your. It's time to clean the field of your entire team roster - young, old or in the past.

Is it done? Are you standing tall? Alone? Good. Set all your luggage down and just breathe. (If anyone tries to sneak on again, just put them back. It may take a few times, but they'll get the picture soon.)

Now, let's talk about your team. Let's talk about how you, and you alone, are a power play.

Take a look across the field to the other side - where your

opposing team awaits. Take a good look at them. Study them. Not one player is like the other, right? They take a lot of different forms and shapes, don't they? Some are people, some are wounds, and some are strangers, laws, requirements and... Let's face it, some are dark. Imagine them all there on the other side, standing a few feet apart from one another.

Now imagine your side again. You're standing in the middle of the turf. Alone. The rest is open and empty grass. You can practically feel the cold wind whipping around you already now, yes? You can nearly taste the echo of the hollow that is around you.

But when I look down from the stands of your stadium, I see something much different.

I see *all* of you out there.

I see many of you. All wearing the same uniform. All wearing the same colors. You too come in many different shapes and sizes. I see every single piece, side and dimension of you standing to attention next to you, behind you - in every direction.

You are not alone. You are comprised of an amazing amount of teammates. There are many of them, and they are all yours. You were born with them. Born with them for the sole purpose of *winning*. You were born to play this game and win it. You just have to know how to do it.

Unfortunately, unless you've actually seen, experienced or acknowledged these parts of you, they won't be on that field with you. You won't be able to see them. I can see them because I've met them in myself by now. I use all my teammates every single day. I know I still have a few to meet, but those I do know and use, I know well. So I can see them in you, even if you can't see them yet.

In my experience, the more people you have on your list, the fewer the number of your *own* teammates have you ever actually met. It makes sense. If you've been using somebody else's skill or talent in an area of your life, that skill or talent may reside in you, but it never has a chance to appear. It's never invited onto your field. It's ignored. It's invisible.

Oh how often I hear people say that they lack skills or that they aren't good at certain things. I hear this much more today than I ever have before. But then I see all these signs in them that alert me, like a big huge flag, that they have skills. I try to tell them, but they simply don't believe.

Part of this, I think, is because we are so focused on ourselves or so wrapped up in our own worlds, that we overlook others. Think about how you discovered your own skills or your own talents. Somebody pointed them out to you or you saw someone doing it and knew you could do the same.

So few people, even teachers, have given up trying to awaken each others skills and teammates. But your teammates are the key. The key to everything.

The best way to win, and I mean *really* win this game of life, is to meet all of your own teammates. All of them. Short, tall, wide and small. Meet them. Then train them. Strengthen them. Get them ready for the field. Make them great players.

It takes time. It takes experience. But the more teammates you meet, the more you will train and the more your body will feel safe enough to introduce you to some more. It's exciting. It's fascinating and it's very, very encouraging. Empowering. Winning.

The larger your team, the stronger your team, the more experienced, trained and independent your team is the better shot they have at not only winning the game, but enjoying the play it takes to get there. Do not compromise. Keep your team straight. Make the hardest cut. Enjoy the greatest of rewards.

Look at your team now. Imagine all the teammates you have. There are so many. They are all wearing your team colors. They are all you. They are so unique, so talented, so different and so strong. Meet them. See them. Get to know them. Then use them.

You are not alone. You have a full field. Keep the others in the stands. Keep yourself on that field. Go out there and play. Take on the force of the opposing team. Take them on. Tell them to bring it. Get ready to defeat them... and the bell will toll.

Adventure awakens.
Your horizons expand.
The touchdowns begin.
And so do the wins.

It gets dirty. It gets rough. There's mud.
It's football.

It's messy. It's precise. It's fast and it is slow. It's amazing. Absolutely amazing. And you have a choice. We all have a choice.

Every single one of us. No matter who we are or where we live, we all have a choice.

To play.
Or not to play.
To win.
Or not to win.
To live.
Or not.

I choose the latter. Will you join me?

4 THE SIDELINES

So you've chosen to live. Wonderful. Your bravery will grow with every word you read. I'm so excited for you!

Making the difficult decision to keep everyone and everything but you and your inherent skills on your field is not easy. But that is not to say that you have to live life alone. Not at all. We are built for community.

You've heard the studies, where the babies who aren't touched wilt quickly. Then there is the importance placed on our teenage years - the vital period of time in which we learn social skills with those outside our immediately family system. It's the time we start to spread our wings a bit and learn how to relate with our friends, our peers and other social communities.

No, we are not built for empty stadiums. It's almost impossible to do, actually, which is why this chapter is so important. The skill of keeping the people in your life in the best possible part of the stadium for you and for them is essential. Keep them in the wrong place and you may never make a touchdown again - even if it's just one person.

Underestimating the power of placements is one of the easiest downfalls we can make. This caution doesn't just apply to your roster - it applies to your whole stadium. Never assume that compromising a single position for anyone anywhere in your stadium can't cost you. It can. It absolutely can. And it does. So very, very often, it does.

So let's look at the four most important roles which hug the playing field. There are four different ones: the head coach, assistant coaches, cheerleaders and spectators. I'd like you to get to know these sections, their characteristics and their roles... and know them well. The better you know them, the easier it is to keep your stadium a healthy and exciting place to be.

- Coming of Age -

The concept of a coach for daily living in our culture is not new. We have business coaches, marriages coaches and even parenting coaches. Then there are those who are close to us that help us, mentor us - coach us when things get tough and rough.

All of us can think of people who played some sort of "coaching" role in lives. Much of that concept applies to your stadium too. And, just as in football, your coaches should be the most important roles that surround your field.

But since we're talking about coaches that will help us win in our adult lives, let's talk first about the coaches we have before then. The coaches we have before the age of 18 greatly affect the rest of our lives and very much shape our stadiums, so let's see exactly how it all lays out before we move on to our next section.

You see, your team doesn't actually take the field for its first official game until you are an adult. For most of us, that's the age of 18. In some cultures "coming of age" happens much earlier. Either way, it's on your first day of adulthood that you finally take the field and play a real game.

On that day, your team, your coaches, your spirit team and your bleachers are all handed over to you and are now underneath your purview. It's the first time you play your entire opposing team instead of just parts of it - and it's also the first time when the consequences of what happens on that field play out in every area of your life.

Before you are an adult, you don't have much of a choice when it comes to coaches. We were designed to be raised by others - helped, formed and trained by those who have gone before us and who know what it is we need to learn before taking that field on our first day of adulthood.

The older you are, the stronger you become, especially in your teenage years. Those are the years you are playing a lot of scrimmage games. You're trying out the skills you've been given and shaping them, honing them and improving them before you are out there on your own, making your own touchdowns with your own coaches.

All of your training before you are an adult is vital and pivotal and has an incredible amount of power over us for the rest of our lives. Especially when it comes to your core training. That's the training you receive between the day you were born straight through to the age of four.

The days of your core training weave the majority of the wiring in your brain. This book, and the life that you live - whether it's winning or losing, tells you a lot about whether that wiring was good or bad. The great news, whatever the wiring you've been given, is that it is not permanent.

You can overcome faulty wiring if you know a thing or two about wires, yes? And boy, do I ever know a thing or two about those! You're going to love it. It's just around the corner.

But for now, we're ready to move on to the coaches you have when you are an adult. The ones you get to choose: your assistant coaches.

- Your Assistant Coaches -

Assistant coaches, by definition, are instructors of a specific area of a sport. If you're familiar with football, or sports in general, you know that there's usually more than one assistant coach per team, especially when it comes to a team with its own stadium. Those teams have head coaches, assistant coaches, managers and even owners. It can be a little overwhelming keeping them all straight at times, and the power rightly balanced - but that's what successful teams need sometimes.

This also rings true when it comes to your own stadium. The larger your team, the more successful it is, the more support you will seek and utilize along the way.

But no matter where you are in life, your team always has room for improvement and growth. That's where the assistant coaches come in. Yes, your head coach is also involved, but we'll get into that role in a moment.

Now, your assistant coaches, just as in football, are not permanent positions. Their number can grow and expand, or shrink and stay small. But most don't stay forever. Many of them come in and out of our lives for just a season or two.

Think about it - the older we grow, so does our team. The longer our team is out there on the rough and tumble field of life, we change. Assistant coaches effect these changes. They are affected by them too. That's the beauty of assistant coaches. They visit, they stay and they coach us in the things we don't know.

These assistant, or "visiting" coaches can come in the form of mentors, big brothers, sponsors, our elders, our doctors, professors, therapists, accountants, bosses and more. They can be family, aunts and uncles, older brothers or sisters and even, from time to time a parent. Keeping parents close to your sidelines as an adult, especially as part of the coaching staff, is both risky and tricky. Take a great amount of care here.

Assistant coaches are in the business of helping parts of your team get stronger. Stronger enough to play the game better and on their own, without the assistant coach doing it for them.

This is a very important thing to keep in mind. Assistant coaches *do not* offer up their own team members as a way of making your team better. Assistant coaches don't get on that playing field with you. They are not members of your team. They are not designed to grab the ball for you - they want to see you do it.

Here is the second and more important thing to remember: all of them, absolutely all of them, should only be there by your request. If they push themselves upon you - push you to keep them close to your team, close to your sidelines, to be part of your coaching team without your own request, then you have a problem.

Actions like this means that at least some of their team members are playing for your opposing team. They won't see it that way. They think they know what's best for you and your team. But anyone who would rather take your ball and make the touchdown for you is just someone who wants to steal the ball from you. And that, my friends, is the very definition of "opposing team."

It's a hard lesson to learn, but learn it. Keep a lookout. It happens to everyone. And knowing it, seeing it and watching for it will be a lifesaver.

Again, these supporting coach positions, just as in football, are never permanent. The coaching staff is and always will be at your discretion. You are now an adult. It is your stadium. It is your team. Your game. Your life. It's lived by you. And nobody else.

Keep it that way, and the sage advice of those who have been there before you, who have seen more than you have, who have lived life on their own and are healthy and whole... they will teach you, show you, instruct you and uphold you. You will meet teammates you never knew you had. You will learn how to heal when certain teammates get hit and you will know how to dodge the opposing team quicker than ever before.

Great assistant coaches are hard to find, but they are better than gold. They will keep that ball in your possession. Treat them right and hear them out. They want your team to win. And even better, they want you to win on your *own*. What in the world is sweeter than that?

If you don't have them, get them. The first one will be the hardest to find, but the rest will come more easily. Then there are those who have been there all along, just waiting for you to ask. Good assistant coaches are cool like that. In the meantime, keep your eyes and heart open for those with a bit of wisdom out there. It's a good place to start.

- Your Head Coach -

In sports, a team's head coach overlooks everything from a team's training to its support system and care. They know how to teach it all, train it all and handle it all. They look out for your team mentally, physically, emotionally. They oversee and sometimes intercede with the coaching and training of every member of their team by the assistant coaches.

A head coach is aware of its team's weaknesses and strengths. A head coach talks to the whole team and knows each one of his or her players extremely well. A good head coach keeps his eye on everything, is watchful, patient and curious. He's humble enough to know when he doesn't have the answers and is wise enough to seek help from outside sources.

So who is your head coach? Who overlooks and chooses the assistant coaches who will be caring for your team? You may have already guessed it by now. It's you.

From the day you step into adulthood, you're not only on the field playing the game, but you're also on the sidelines. You are the head coach. Actually, you are more than just the head coach. You are the manager, the team captain *and* the head coach. Once again.

You are the big head honcho. Yes. You are *it*.

The beauty and the beast of adulthood and having your own vast stadium is that you are the main guy - the director - the decider - the manager... the 'master & commander' of sorts.

This is because it is YOU who is out there on that field. You. And you need to be able to pick and choose who takes care of your team, spends time with your team and influences your team. In order for you to do that, you have to be all three rolled into one: manager, head coach, captain.

For some of you I hope this is good news. You've been trampled on enough. For others, please don't think of it as bad news. Once you are in charge, you're able to do a lot less work, believe it or not. Working for others - for another team captain or another manager... wow. It's exhausting. You were meant - yes, you were *built* to be both your team and your team captain. It's true.

It's hard at first. It's work. It's responsibility. But it's true.

So many people will tell you otherwise. So many people will tell you this is not possible. They are wrong.

In order for you to play, run and work hard, like an oiled machine, and win your games instead of lose them; you must *not* be in the habit of handing over the reigns to others. Not in marriage, not in church, not anywhere.

Oh now, don't get riled up, my friends. I'm not being blasphemous - do I sound like a blasphemous person? No. He's my guy and I promise you that one day, I will write about Him and the team He's given us. I will. In the meantime I have a little note about it at the end of this chapter, for those who are interested. Anyhow. Back to it.

Handing over the keys to your team to anyone else, even something else, is death.

It's the dangerous, deadly and sure-fire way to keep the scoreboard clean of any victories for you and your team.

- Your Cheer Squad -

This one is a bit easier. I'm pretty sure you know exactly who your cheerleaders are for your life, or at least you have an idea. Knowing who loves you can be difficult, or who cares for you or who hurts for you can be even more difficult and even fuzzy at times too. The substance that we call love is so very... *blendable*.

But who cheers for you? This squad roster isn't so hard to

figure out. Well, not completely. There are some things to look out for and be aware of.

First, we all need cheerleaders. Only a few will do, but a life without them is hard. They make a difference. They help us make those touchdowns, especially when we are being pushed back, trounced or piled upon.

I've heard people say that when times were tough, their friends disappeared. They'd say, "I found out who my real friends were." I've been through devastating times too, and learned a lot about my friends as well. But man, it's a hard thing do, sticking around when things are rough for someone.

Let's be really honest here. The fact of the matter is that it's really hard to sit in a stadium watching a team lose. It just is. By the time they make it all the way to the third quarter, they've seen too much for too long. They just want to look away... to go home.

In my experience, not everyone is able to handle all that life dishes out to each of us. But some are. There are many kinds of cheerleaders in this world, and yes, their gift is being able to cheer for your team, without asking for anything in return and despite any score you may have on your board.

The interesting thing about cheerleaders, I find, is that they don't necessarily have to be close to you. Some of the most amazing cheerleaders in my life weren't my best friends or even relatives. Life is funny that way. Oh yes, those closer to you can be cheerleaders as well, but sometimes, when we're close to the situation, we can't help but want to play the assistant coach position rather than simply the cheerleader one.

But that's all we need sometimes. A nod of the head, or a nice big chant or a full on loud-n-proud cheer, with waves and leaps and pom-poms... The power of each is so unique. It's not the same as a parent's pat on the back, or a friend's sympathy flowers. The Cheerleading squad somehow catapults you higher - to your best - in some strange sort of joyful magic we were built to need.

So choose you cheerleaders wisely. You don't have to let them in to any huddle. You don't have to share your life story. You just have to be receptive. And thankful. And yes, a lot of cheerleaders don't wait for us to pick them. They just cheer for us anyway. Our choice is to let that cheer warm our hearts or bounce off of us and fade.

Too many of us have a hard time being open to having them in our lives, in our stadium and near our fields. But just imagine a football team playing without them. Alone. A team with an empty stadium. That team just wouldn't play the same. So don't forget to include this squad.

Without them, you can win. Absolutely. But it'll be much harder to do. Period.

- Your Spectators -

Your spectators are the people in the stands. Depending on where and what games you go to, they are also called the bleachers or simply 'the seating.' This is where most of the people in your life will be. It's also where everyone else sits too, which makes this section a different beast altogether.

You see, as coach and captain, you have a say as to who steps onto the field's level. You can kick anyone off there you want to. Coaches, visitors, team members, cheerleaders - they are all there because you allow them to be. It's important to cultivate your field choices and choose wisely, but that's it. That power ends once you hit the stands- or at least the nosebleed section. You don't get to control who is up there. Not in the game of life. Not completely.

Anyone can buy a ticket to your game. You'd have to be a hermit in the mountains to keep the crowds away from your stadium. It's becoming even harder in the digital and social media world as more and more strangers start to crowd your seats, for any myriad of reasons - from mental instability, to curiosity, to envy, to research and money.

Thankfully you do have options. There are choices you can make.

For example, every stadium has a security team, and yours does as well. Your security team, which is made up of your own teammates, is able to seat people close to you or far away from you. In some instances, you're able to kick them out altogether, as I mentioned earlier in this chapter. Again, that it a very difficult thing to do but it can be done.

You also get to choose who sits in your "front row." There was an essay once written about our "front row" long ago. The ones you find online are much different from the original. Those have the same tone or empathy the original did, nor the wisdom, compassion and insight.

Still, we do have a front row in our stadiums and it does matter who we allow to sit there. How you keep these front rows safe and the rest of the seating spaced accordingly is also up to your security team... and a little thing called 'boundaries.' Those have a whole book of their own. I'm serious. There's an actual book out there with the title *Boundaries* and everything.

But the point is - just because some one wants to be a part of your life doesn't mean they have to be. You have a choice as to how close they are to you while you're playing out there on the field.

As for social networking, you have choices there too. Keeping your life safe online isn't easy, but it can be done. There will be sacrifices, and it truly is up to you, the head coach, to decide whether it is worth it or not.

Now, here is a rather remarkable lesson I have learned on the road to building my winning team. It never ceases to shock me, this one, but it has held true over time. I've seen it happen in so many other lives, that I can't help but share it with you. It makes perfect sense once you think about it, but still, it's surprising how little we are aware of it.

Here it is: how you play affects who comes to see you play. If you get stronger and start winning, people who secretly loved watching you lose will leave your stands. It will hurt your feelings. You never suspected that's why they watched, though, so you will think you are doing something wrong. You might even think you must not be winning since people are leaving.

Don't ever think that. After a while, new people will start entering your stands. The ones who like seeing a team play the smart way, the strong way and the healthy way. If we play so that our own members of our own team have the ball at all times, people who play the same way will come to cheer you on.

Be prepared. The bottom line here? The more we grow and change, the more the demographics of our stadium attendees change.

You'll even see people's careers change when they get better at their game, or you'll notice that they are suddenly talking differently about their job or coworkers. Companies are types of stadiums too. If they have bad habits, they often attract those who play with those same bad habits in their own lives. If a company is cutting corners or the owner is smarmy, then the employees will tend to be the same types of persons or turn into those types the longer they stay.

It's fascinating. It's enlightening. Like attracts like. So if you change, expect to see a change in those around you. It's not a bad thing. It's a sign of something good.

So there we have it: our head coach, our assistant coaches, our cheerleading team and our spectators. Since we ourselves are the head coach, there's only three other roles your friends and family belong, and once you discover where they fit, your relationships with them will deepen, grow and blossom. As will the numbers on your scoreboard.

- Side Note -
What About Faith?

This book is written for believers and non-believers alike. This short side note is for the believers and/or people in recovery who are doing their steps. Now. You might be asking yourselves where to put your Higher Power in your stadium. He is there. Sometimes I think He is my team's owner, in that I turn to Him to ask what to do next. Quite often, though, He wants me to speak up about my own desires. Then we go back and forth.

But see, owners don't do that. They don't wait on a coach to ask first before giving directions. No - He is simply my creator. In the early years of my faith I wanted Him to be my head coach - desperately. I wanted Him to be my captain even. I wanted all the decisions, all the ideas, all the choices to be His. I wanted Him on my field, making all of the plays. Instead, He came alongside and helped flush out my team - helped me learn all the lessons in this book. That's why I'm sharing it with you. So no, I am not deleting Him, but I am most definitely playing for Him.

5 THE LOCKER ROOM

Knowing where we need to be in life and actually living it are two very different things. The hurdles that most of us face, without realizing it, have to do with the people in our lives. Their wants, their needs, what we think they need and what we think they want, are all things we tend to give priority to rather than the game at hand.

But this is life, and life isn't that easy or simple. There are other large and significant barriers that take time and a bit of experience to spot. But we'll never spot them unless your crowd clears. You'll never see them unless it's just you and your team facing off on that field with your opposing team.

Just imagine a football game with more than two teams out there - if one of the teams started using members from other teams. Those members, of course, are wearing their own colors. Can you imagine the chaos that would ensue down there on that playing field? Can you imagine being one of the players down there?

The game comes into focus once there are only two teams with two different colors on a football field. The same goes for you. To play a straight, powerful and successful game, you need to move everyone else in your life off the playing field. You need to shift them into the sections that free you up to finally play your own game for once.

Hopefully having meaningful places in the rest of the stadium to move them into helps you to actually move them there. It's always difficult to make such positive changes in our lives without others feeling the shift. But that doesn't make it wrong. That doesn't make it unhealthy. That doesn't negate healing.

What wound can heal without the pain of cleaning it first? Know these shifts of yours won't damage others - in reality it almost always helps them to live more successful lives too, but that should *never* be our goal. Our own stadium and its health should be at the heart of every move.

It's the way we were designed. We were all designed to do something on this earth, but we must be healthy to do it. If we are not healthy, if we are not winning, then we are only crippled - too handicapped to truly make any mark, or difference for that matter, in this world.

If you've already made the "hardest cut" or have done this kind of work before, take a moment to look back and think on the differences. Think of those who filled unhealthy roles in your stadium. How many of them were on your field instead of off it? How many had authority over you, playing your head coach instead of standing back and cheering for you? Are they watching you now and cheering you on? Do they really want you to win without them?

Now we have better and healthier places to put them in our hearts and in our minds. Now we have a chance to breathe our own air, make our own decisions and feel out our true options. We can finally see which problems are ours and not others. We can finally sit down, relax and take a good look at what we're left with: us.

Ourselves. Our own teams. It's time to meet them and get to know them. What better place than in our own locker room? Yes, I said locker room.

- Your Locker Room -

We all have a locker room, where we go to regroup, re-strategize, heal and think. There is a reason half-time exists. Teams would be a disaster without a locker room to head back to, get ready in and do everything else they need to do to prepare for a huge event that takes a toll physically, mentally and emotionally.

Can you imagine everyone just showing up on the field, dressed and ready to go? No talking to each other? No spending time together? No processing, strategizing or planning? No time to take a breath during a game and seriously reconsider where everything stands? No way.

For us a locker room isn't a physical place. It's more of a state of mind, really. It's the time you take to process, heal and think through things. Most of us can do this in a variety of places. What's important is that you take time to do it.

Think of if at the time you spend with your team. Remember, your team has a lot of different moving parts. Physical things like cars and robots need a lot of care and maintenance. It's the same with your team. The time you take to maintain your team and your teammates is considered your locker room.

You locker room can come in all shapes and sizes. They are as different as we are. Where do you regroup? Where do you re-strategize, heal and think? Where to you reflect inward. When do you process the day - the conversations, the arguments, and the work week?

I do a lot of my processing and healing on the road. I just take off in my car and drive... drive, drive, drive. I explore. I think, then stop to take pictures that inspire me, and then I talk, because I love taking Nick with me on these drives. We both grow together. And we both love learning about our teammates.

I also write in my journal. I have a million of them, tucked into different corners of the house, car and luggage. I don't keep just one. I just want one close, so I can write when I need to. Again, the act of physically putting pen to paper changes you. It's a powerful place to rest and rejuvenate in your locker room.

Libraries, hikes, airplanes, quiet times, lunch breaks - we all have a locker room available to us. We just have to choose one. Some of you already use them. Do you use that time to get to know more of your teammates? Try it. When you do take the time to rest, to contemplate or to process, then you'll probably know more of your teammates than you think you do and you're probably more open to meeting some new ones.

If you don't know many of your teammates, then it's a pretty good bet that you don't spend much time in your locker room. It's always there - you just have to use it. It's the only place where you will ever meet or discover any of your teammates that you didn't already know about before adulthood.

And I'm not talking your one year checkup here either. We are much more complicated than any machine. We need daily, weekly and monthly recharges, examinations and lessons. Meditate if you have to, journal if you have to or find someone who will listen if you have to.

So many of us who make sure to take daily care of others instead ourselves don't realize the difference between help from a losing team and help from a winning team. And there's a big difference. A really big one. Find your locker room and start investing some time in it. You have a lot of teammates just waiting to meet you there.

- My Original Team -

To help you better understand what your locker room looks like, as well as understand who your possible teammates are, I'm going to introduce you to my original team. This is the team I walked into adulthood with. When I was 18 and off to college, this is the team I had on the field. Once you meet them, you'll understand why I borrowed so many other team members to survive my adult life.

Just like I said, borrowing other people's teammates didn't work. I didn't make it very far into adulthood before crumbling. I think 'imploding' would be a better term for it. I had horrible coaches growing up. By the time I was thrown into the world of adults, I was a mess. My team wasn't just weak. It was broken. Off balance. Missing pieces. So many pieces!

My teammates, the ones I knew only a very little about, didn't work well together at all. Every day of my adulthood was a major struggle. It took pokes and prods from people around me to figure out where the scrimmage line was, never mind knowing that there was another team on the field - one that was there to take me down.

It was terrible.

Let's go back in time... into my locker room on my 18th birthday. I'm using 18 as a reference, like I said before, though I personally feel I was shoved onto the field of adulthood at 15. Maybe at birth. My husband was shoved into it very early on. I wonder what age *you* were thrown into adulthood? It's something to think about, truly.

Either way, let's take a peek into the locker room of my former life.

The Captain

I knew I was the head of the team - my conscious self. Though everyone on my team now was also on my team then, I certainly didn't acknowledge or rely upon all of them like I do now. I relied on just a few team members to survive and used them over and over and over again without any rest.

Sadly, I didn't like a lot of my other team members, so I consistently stole or borrowed other people's team members to make me feel like I had a good team to play with. I'd go onto the field much more confident when I had someone else's team members out there next to me. They all seemed so much stronger than my own players. Wiser.

I felt like my personal teammates were aberrations - problems to be handled. I did everything in my power to keep the ones I knew about from playing. I thought they would cost me the game. I was terrified of playing the wrong way, of failing, of bringing shame upon my head. That fear probably paralyzed my ability as the captain more than anything.

Instinct

He was a small little player who looked really brainy and pushy and strong. I really didn't like him at all. At *all*. My coaches had warned me that he was really selfish and full of sin. If I knew anything, I knew *never* to talk to him. I tried to put duct tape over his mouth, actually, but really, he just fought harder. He was an incredibly strong teammate.

I finally gave up and just tried to hide from him.

The opposing team loved tackling him for me though. I always thought they were my friends because of it. As far as I was concerned, I was embarrassed my Instinct even existed. When he jumped up and down I would flood with shame. The red of the shame would pour from the very crown of my head down my hands, feet, face and body...

But there's was nothing I could do about him. Instinct would just endlessly jump up and down, trying to shout through the tape, refusing to lay low or be hidden in any way shape or form. I could almost make out what he was saying too - he was just that good. But I did finally learn to tune him out. That took a lot of practice though.

Eventually I just let him. I'd let him jump and jump and jump - even expected it half the time, but would ignore him as he did it. I'd just stare at him, numb, motionless, waiting for him to finish. That really seemed to work, and I pretty much stuck with it. He knew he wasn't mama's favorite, but then again, he really didn't seem to care either, which, again, just frustrated and angered me. As much as I could feel those two emotions anyway.

Instinct was the ass in the locker room. That's how I saw him. The annoyance. The embarrasser. I really, *really* wished he'd been kicked off the team at birth!

But Instinct turned out to be my most valuable player. There is a writer who says that we are the most deeply wounded in the place that our genius lays. I've found that to be true. Took a tremendous amount of time to learn though. What a smart play by the opposing team, don't you think?

Anger

You know what did happen at birth? I am so sad to say this, knowing all that I know now, but Anger was literally bound, gagged, chained and stuffed into a small metal box and shoved behind one of the lockers literally days after I was born. I didn't know he existed.

I'd heard tales of him from others from time to time, but it was usually through the looking glass of stage plays, cop shows and my peer counseling training. I didn't know he was designed to be an asset. I never knew he was valuable. I thought he was a sin. So I never looked for him. Never sought him out.

I did meet Anger's older brother, Rage, though, through my father. Let's just say my father had... episodes. When Rage took over my dad's own team and beat us, broke us, and did what was necessary to scare us, even scare mom while she watched him terrorize us, I would freeze. Go numb. Like playing dead.

It didn't happen very often, not that I can remember, but I do know that I always thought of Rage when people mentioned Anger. I suppose that's why I never considered him to be part of any of us... I thought he was an aberration... an event... a crime.

I never thought Anger was, could be and is, a valuable and essential part of my team, never mind anyone else's. He is. He's vital. I'm so thankful I know better now. He sits on the bench now, since he's still recovering from the chains he wore for decades, and it hurts when he finally gets to take the field.

When we're done playing, I usually have to nurse his wounds. But he always scores. It took time, but he always scores. I'll be honest though, I'm years into knowing Anger and he still isn't that strong. He surely isn't in the shape he was designed for. I get upset at this now. I am angry because I still can't play Anger the way he was meant to be played.

Fear

Fear was my right hand man. He was always with me. In fact, I think he was team captain most of the time, not me. Fear managed everything in my life - everything! Always. In every single way. I knew Fear so well I'd forget he wasn't the only part of me. I remember hearing the cheesy quotes, "there's nothing to fear, but fear itself" and I'd scoff, thinking there was absolutely nothing to be afraid of when it came to Fear.

I had no idea how incredibly afraid I was every single moment of every single day. I was well into adulthood when I experienced my first day without Fear at the helm. It was as if someone had flipped up the shade in a dark room and was high noon outside.

Back then though, Fear had the ability to prevent bad things from happening. Fear was always on alert, ready to come flying in at any moment. It was always at the ready because it was always, always, always needed. It warned me to stop, draw back, contract. Like a turtle into its shell.

Sometimes Fear was really bad for my health though. Sometimes I couldn't breathe, sometimes I'd have a panic attack and sometimes, the worst times, I'd sit trembling, shaking from head to toe, in my bed dreading... something. I didn't even know what. But sleep was not an option. Only Terror, Fear's big brother, would sit at the foot of my bed, rocking me back and forth, back and forth, with not a moment of relief in sight.

I still remember those nights. I still try to figure out exactly what I was afraid of. All I remember is Terror, sitting right next to me in my bed, his terrible arm wrapped around me, refusing to let go.

Caution

Holy Mole! Was my Caution the best and biggest guy on the team or what? Oh man, Caution handed me so many successes. He was really, really watchful, always in the front - one of my absolute best players. My Coaches didn't train him, they mostly focused on Fear, but as an unintended consequence, they gave Caution a workout on the side.

I walked into adulthood knowing I was the best at avoiding conflict of any kind on any level in any atmosphere.

Caution was my knight in shining armor. He did an awesome job of beating back Intuition when he tried to speak up. Caution always told me to expect all the options - and that usually meant all the bad options - so I was always ready when things turned south, no matter where I was. My Creativity got quite a work out too, actually. She's amazing at conjuring up every imaginable and terrible scenario you can think of. I'd be prepared for all of it.

The only drawback to Caution was that when something went well, I was surprised. Off guard. In shock. Upset. I never handled awards well. I received a lot of my final year of school because I'd done such a great job of avoiding conflict at home (grades), with my siblings (after school activities) and in my church (an immense amount of public service and mission projects), that I was very happy to have survived.

But to receive rewards for it? I had no team players for that. At least, none that were let out of their boxes and chains yet. So instead, not knowing what to do, I panicked and did what I knew how to do best - threw Fear out there on the field.

He always confused people, I know, but I didn't know who else to play! So my memories of getting all of those awards are all combined with the confused, concerned and baffled looks of those giving them to me.

Looking back I can now understand what their faces were saying, "She doesn't feel any ownership or pride for her work? Then why did she do any of it?" Many of those who gave out the awards had never met me before. They were surprised when they saw me. I looked so contracted - not confident, not bold.

Some even gave me looks of disgust for it. Those I understood. Those I believed I deserved. I'm so sad for all of us who were robbed of our most precious team members by our abusive and intrusive, violent coaches - who hurt us instead of protected us. I'm sad we could not enjoy our rewards and I'm even sadder that we were robbed of a childhood. Every child deserves the taste of joy in their mouths, instead of rot.

Knowledge

Oh Knowledge, who I liked okay, but only because I had to. I didn't really see his potential in the game as a whole. Knowledge was "school" and knowledge was "memorizing" and Knowledge was the teammate that either beat someone or lost to them. There was no in between.

I didn't like Knowledge for this. I hated the egoism of my classmates... I saw what memorizing and quoting and referring things meant. It meant you were either smart or dumb. I didn't see the many gifts and talents that also constituted smarts. I only saw winning and losing. And I wasn't allowed to lose.

Knowledge didn't play a part in my real life, my off-campus life, I felt - only my school life. Knowledge could garner good grades, but nothing more. Surprisingly, it was the same in church. I was raised in a church who absolutely founded its praise upon one's ability to know what to do and how to do it the exact right, specific and reverential way in order to... I don't know... pass?

Yes, Knowledge was a necessary player for survival, but I did not consider it my friend. I did not know its value once I graduated. I did not seek its insight for my players.

Perspective

Perspective was a total favorite of mine. He and I would totally debate with each other, back and forth, inside and around, and quite often, loved meeting and playing with other teams.

Perspective is the one player I never traded. Perspective is the one player I've trained since I can remember, and who I've never stopped training. I love Perspective. I love the world's he opens for me, and Perspective, I feel like, wants me in the end zone all the time. I love him so much, and I feel like he was born strong in my team.

I think back and wonder why Perspective wasn't kept locked up by my coaches. And I see that they tried to - they just didn't know who Perspective was. They thought my words, my ideas and my "perspectives" weren't a gift, but something either from school or me simply being "loud."

They most definitely went after the "loud" part. They hated it when I opened my mouth. In that way, they hindered me from speaking my Perspective in the house, but see... Perspective kept going in the silence. He's not based on whether he's heard or not. So they missed their opportunity.

Thankfully UCLA wanted me to open my mouth. They loved my Perspective and wanted to hear from him all the time. I'm grateful for Perspective. I believe he fuels a lot of my writing. He fuels a lot of my stories. And he most definitely makes a lot of my friends laugh. Perspective and I, we have always been good friends.

Intuition

Then there is Intuition, who, like a ghost, plays even when I tell him not to. He gets me into trouble all the time! If he sees a field goal, he'll grab the ball and kick it, before I can even grab him and stop him, yelling, "But I don't *want* to win against this person!!!" But yeah. Intuition kicks it anyway. And snickers at me as he walks on by back to the locker room, satisfied he's won a game.

Intuition, by the way, is the most highly sought after player of mine. People want to steal him all the time. Perspective too. They work hand in hand by the way, though, like I said, Intuition is just a naughty little sneak who got me in trouble all the time. People don't like a smarty-pants, and my lovely guy Intuition always had a knack for making me one, which, darn it, made for all those confrontations I was trying to avoid. And, can't you tell? I tried to avoid *all* confrontations, even ones that only measured .00018 on the Richter scale.

Oi. Intuition was a pain. He still is, from time to time, but only because he scares me - scares my husband too. For example, I was listening to the radio today and a journalist was testing a computer that's said to read minds. It turned out that the computer could read minds. It repeated back exactly the word the journalist had said, letter by letter.

The real scary part? That I said the word before the computer had the chance to spell it into the microphone. No, I hadn't heard the story before and no, the journalist didn't tell us the word first. I just knew it. And said it. And then the computer did. Which means I'm faster than a computer at reading people's minds. Aah! Like I said, my Intuition can be a pain!

This is the kind of stuff that makes me want to drive off the road in shock. Maybe you don't call that Intuition. Maybe you call that something else. But it's not enjoyable to have.

Feel my pain for a moment. The last time I watched Star Wars, and poor old Ben Kenobi doubled over in pain from feeling an entire planet being destroyed on the other side of the universe, I dropped my plate and stared. I'd been letting Intuition run free lately and new things had started happening. Like this doubling-over-from-a-universe-away type maneuver.

I whispered, "Oh my God... that's *me!*" Did my company feel my shock? Did they pat their hands on my back or shoulder and make me feel better? Did they even do me the great honor of saying, "Girl, you're nuts! That's science *fiction!*"

No. No, no, no. They looked up from their game, saw the screen, and started dying with laughter. They were high five-ing. One nearly lost himself crying. And all I kept hearing was... "That *is* you!!!!" in the middle of many high pitched hysterics. No empathy. No sympathy. I think they even backed the movie up a little to play it again.

Yeah? You try it.

Stupid Intuition. I love your little butt. And hate it too.

———

Ah, there are more teammates on my team, but these paint quite the accurate painting for you. I think we've all got the picture here, right? Let's move on a bit.

- Types of Teammates -

I hope this portrait of my original team helped you understand or see your own team, teammates and locker room a bit. We have all been born with different kinds of tools, and the way we are raised shapes and molds those tools. Some were locked up and hidden from you. Others were developed more than the rest.

But when we are adults, we get to call all of them out of their closets and into the middle of the room - and you suddenly have a whole new team. You have so many more options, ways and abilities to become the indestructible team you were designed to be.

Considering most of us don't know all of our teammates though, let me throw out some areas in which most of us have been given numerous teammates, whether we are aware of them or not. Let's start with the following common types of teammates:

- Our Emotions (fear, joy, anger)
- Inherent Skills (intuition, caution, etc)
- Mental Skills (math, verbal, spatial, wit, etc)
- Physical Abilities & Attributes (height, weight, muscles, etc)
- Spiritual (giving, teaching, prophecy, etc)

As you can see, you have a lot of team members. More than you expected, right? Do you see your side of the field filling up? More team members make for a greater win. And even better, when we strengthen one player, other players usually benefit from it and gain strength as well. The more team members we pay attention to, and actually discover, the better the whole team works, and is able to help strengthen and affect the other members.

We don't all have the same skills, of course. For example, I am highly spatial and my husband is highly sequential. We are both gifted and strong, but he can't tell which way he entered a parking lot and I can't figure out how much change I owe. I could, at any point in the day, tell you where we are on a map and the streets, cities and counties surrounding us. He can do advanced multiplication in a matter of seconds. My spatial teammate is much stronger than Nick's, and his sequential teammates can take mine own down.

Does this mean that they have to be uneven in talent for the rest of our lives? No. I can develop my sequential teammate. I had to when I owned a store-front business. My sequential guy got quite the workout. But he became quite lazy once we had to leave it behind, and I'm okay with that. He's still stronger than he was before, and I am glad for the training.

Nick's spatial gnome of a teammate really despises workouts, or at least, that's what he tells me. In any case, he's developed enough that he can navigate Nick around a ballroom dance floor, but that's about it. Should his work ever require him to develop his little gnome, I have a feeling it would grow three inches. That's just my guess.

Anyhow, the point is that we are all born with teammates that are innately strong and they tend to help us throughout our lives, whether we know it or not. I knew I was spatial, for example, when the only courses of math I excelled in were geometry based. I didn't realize at the time though, that it played such a magnificently larger role in life skills until much, much later on.

It helps me drive, navigate, calculate, measure, cook, bake, pack, stack and storage. My sister always called me the "master packer." I thought that was just a cute name... until I managed to get 23 grocery bags full of food into the back seat of my little Honda civic for a road trip.

Ah. Okay. I've got a kick-ass Spatial guy on my team. Awesome. But I stink at buying a car. Ah well, that's what Nick's for, right? But before I met him I learned I could develop any side of myself - not to his level of brilliance, or anyone else's genius, but my opposing team no longer had an easy win in the areas I chose to develop.

———

Yes, we are all made differently, and I'm discovering that it's one of the best parts of life, discovering how I'm made. After thirty plus years, I've learned, hands down, that I will still be learning things about myself when I'm 80. How awesome is that?

There was a time I would have found that frustrating, but we are fearfully and wonderfully made. I believe that. I see that. And I'm okay with the fact I haven't met all my teammates yet. Because every time I meet one for the first time, so many puzzle pieces fall into places - memories make sense, stories make sense, decisions make sense... my past lines up like dominos. It's a wonderful experience, not a dull one.

And then I get to enjoy using that teammate, welcoming them to the team, and looking out for them when they play - even giving them more opportunities to play. I grow them, train them and enjoy them. It never feels like work. It's edifying, like food for the soul.

Unfortunately, the teammates that we all share - that we all have in equal measure - are most often the ones that society discards. I don't know where or how this practice started but it's been a part of our heritage for far too long.

Let's take, for example, our emotions. We all have them, whether we allow them to actually surface or not. But for some reason they are seen as handicaps - as deterrents to our way of life.

Minimizing these teammates, ignoring them or shaming them, causes so much damage in our lives. From books like *Gift of Fear*, to studies like Plutchik's wheel of emotions, there is a whole world of science that recognizes and stresses the importance of getting to know and using the gifts that are our emotional teammates. And yet we abuse them - shamelessly.

We bury them in beer and escape them in wine. We say they don't exist, then let them out in a vast angry steam called venting. They become our weakness and our one of our greatest sources of fear. We try to mould them, force them and fit them into sociable molded smiles. But it doesn't work. And then we miss out on all that they were created for - like precious red flags being bleached a cold surrendering white.

Let's take a closer look and learn why.

- The Logic of Emotions -

A friend recently told me about her struggles and concerns about some big changes happening in the life of her family, which I found totally legit and well founded. Then she sighed and said, "And then I just realized that all this is just emotions, not fact or reality, so... I need to just let it go." Uh oh.

No. There's no "letting go" of emotions, people. Ever hear the saying, "feelings buried alive never die"? Well learn it. It is ridiculously true. When we don't feel emotions or refuse to feel them, they bury deep in your heart and, like little seeds, start to take root. The more you push an emotion down, the more that root grows.

Then the day comes, as it always does, when it poisons your heart, choking it out. Then the emotion is revealed - it spills out, sometimes explodes out, and the repercussions are so very much more damaging than had we faced and been able to regulate the emotions when they were first "born."

I'll say it again. Feelings buried alive never die. And there's a reason for this. It's because we were designed with emotions. They were given to us as a part of our winning team. Just like wheels on a car, they are necessary to make our teams move forward.

But when left unattended, their roots take hold so deeply and grow so wide that they start breaking through the concrete. Just as roots of a tree break apart even the best roads, so does the fruit of our buried emotions. When we are young, we have the energy to sit down on the tomb that holds all that we felt, but never released, used or burned.

But the older we grow, the more the contents in the tomb grow and the harder it becomes to hold the lid down. We have mid-life crises. We hurt the ones we love. We snap or lash out erratically or we become depressed and inconsolable. We grow older and suddenly dementia appears, defensiveness is everywhere and bam! We can no longer hold any kind of lid down.

The black spills out and, as much as the family tries to hide it, the ugly is blatant. Untamed. Wild.

Some of us were locked up tighter than others, and the tomb split open earlier in life. For some of us, it's during our teenage years. For others it's during the college years. I think the earlier episodes are happening more and more.

I wonder if it's because kids are encouraged to act like cartoons more and more and their programming, books and television promote "silly" more and more. I even saw an "emotions puzzle" once with faces of each emotion on each piece. It was designed for kids. But it had only four emotions on there - and one was literally the word "silly."

Silly is not an emotion. It's a description for the actions of cartoons. Cartoons have no emotions. They are play things. Young. Undeveloped. Ignoring or burying our emotional teammates is one of the most dangerous moves we can teach our children, and yet we are doing it all the time, every single day.

I have learned these lessons especially well. I could not put words to them, though, for so very long. And then all of the lessons clicked into place when one especially talented doctor put it this way: "Don't expect emotions to follow the rules of mental logic. They have their own rules, their own 'logic.' And each set of these two logics, mental and emotional, are both equal in value."

My mind was blown. So much fell into place for me. Emotional Logic literally has its own rules and regulations that are different and set apart from Mental Logic. There is actually a thing called Emotional Logic.

It helps so much. It unveils so much. Both logics, mind and heart, are equally important. We were built with two sets of circuitry to navigate and understand life with, not one. They are the Logical (Mental) and Emotional (Feeling).

What would we ever do without Fear? Shame? Joy? Anger? How much would we miss out on, avoid, save ourselves from and protect ourselves from without the emotional realm within us? In the Myers Briggs personality charts, they also lay out these two forms of logic as equal also - they say we either lean towards being an 'S' - sensing, or an 'F' - feeling. They never! *ever* at any point, list one as being more valuable than the other.

The problem is, it is really, really hard to face our feelings. We as a society have always had an incredibly difficult time feeling, expressing and processing our emotions. We became better at it once upon a time. Even quite good at it. We had an amazing healthy society compared to the generations before us, I think. I feel that as education grew around the world, so did our abilities to admit, acknowledge and face the "other" logic within us that is just as important.

But now we have the web. And true to its name, it's caught us. We don't feel, we don't cope, we don't really exist, even. Every time I go anyplace in California, and watch everyone walking by each other, faces down and into their phones, whether it be a single girl or an entire family... no one is actually "in" the spot they occupy. Only the tourists are. It's fascinating and draining all at the same time.

Every single time I see things like this, it makes me think of the same scene. It replays in my head, for the thousandth time: *The Matrix*. Neo in that clear pod full of pink gelatinous goo made of dead millions - all being harvested for the power they produce. And how do they keep us unaware of our bodies? With The Matrix. The thing we never feel.

Only in this matrix, the one I see when we are all in designer clothing, with our heads tucked into our digital hand hold, we don't supply them with electricity - just our money. You'd be amazed at just how much of their soul people will give up for the illusion that they are Brittney or Cher, Jay-Z or JT, not realizing that in trying to be them, they only feed them. Create them. Pay them. Give them their "energy" they can't survive without.

While their bodies, here on land, wither, waste and... lose.

Ignoring our emotions, my friends, is not just forfeiting to the other team, it's playing for them. And that's just a low down dirty shame. Avoid it. Discover your teammates. All of them. And not only occupy the space you are in, but conquer it.

It's the only way.

6 YOUR OPPOSITION

Of course, the other side has a locker room too. Yes, I said the other side. There is always a team you are playing against and let me tell you one thing: they want you to lose. And lose big.

There is a reason why life is tricky. There's a reason that it's hard. There's an incredibly large amount of hurdles, heights, deserts and landmines that will be thrown, placed or sprawled along your way through your entire adulthood. That's your opposing team.

The bad bosses, the bad health, the bad weather and the bad childhood - they all form one super team that we all, *all* must face. No matter what strata of the economic hemisphere you're born into, this team still stands ready, waiting and wanting to push you further and further away from the goal line your entire life.

Their motto is "know thine enemy," and they take it very, very seriously. We are studied every single moment of every single day. Every nook and every cranny - every weak point, sore spot and trigger- they see it, they memorize it... they *know* us. They know our buttons and yes, yes, yes - do they ever love to push them.

I know you've seen it. The opposing team leaves visible marks upon those they have repeatedly shut out of a win. Worse, you've seen people whose opposing teams have kept them so far away from the end zone, that they have never even seen so much as a blade of its grass.

No nation, language, ethnicity or status is exempt. Every single one of us takes the field with an opposing team.

Not one of us, though, is playing the same team. No one's

opposing team is like another. Your opposing team is made up of a variety of members, and depending on how you're playing, they'll trade in different kinds of players out of the blue to catch you off guard- sometimes they can switch up three different players in one single minute. They are good. Very, very good.

I've had some, quite frankly, historic battles with my opposing team. Those around me who were in my stadium at the time, whether on the sidelines or in the stands, will remember some of those games for the rest of their lives. I certainly will.

Some of those games broke me. I have sustained injuries. I have battle scars. And I have medals. A ton of medals. Or trophies, if you prefer.

Perhaps I'll tell you more about them one day, and you'll most certainly hear about certain parts of them in this book, along with the stories from so many others, who have faced similar things.

Because even though each of our opposing teams is designed for us, they share a lot of similar qualities. Just like you and I have similarities, so do they. I've seen so many opposing teams make the same plays upon us, that I started to see patterns. I made notes. Then I made more notes. I visited more people's stadiums. I gathered more research. I talked and asked questions and started listening. Listening, listening, listening, all the time.

I heard so many things and saw their work in so many lives that I finally threw up my hands, dropped my books and did.... *it*. The unthinkable. I risked it all. I made a run for it. At *them*. I went covert and yes... I broke into their locker room and stole their playbook! Hells yes I did. Grabbed the whole huge darn thing.

Know what I found? They've been making the same plays for centuries. They've been sharing secrets. They've been honing their skills, practicing plays, sharpening their swords and their spears. They've become a bit cocky, actually. And that's our in.

I think it's high time we fight back. I think it's time to train. To take our lives back. To start winning again. To be prepared, not scared, and powerful instead of petty.

It's *on*. We may always have an opposing team, just like we'll always have our own stadium, but it doesn't mean we have to be a losing team. They are just visitors after all. They don't own the stadium. We do. They're on *our* turf. And it's time to let them know it, right? Right. Drum roll please!

- Step One -

Oddly enough, this first step in understanding our opposition is very much like the first step in the Twelve Step communities. Step one in their handbook is accepting that you have a problem. Many people attend several meetings before ever taking the first step. Some people take years.

That's because it's a big step. Admitting there is a monster in the room means that you have actually looked at it. It's a simple 'must' for ever getting it out of the room. But it's easier said than done.

Same here when it comes to our opposing team. Step one for us in this chapter, is admitting that life is hard. That it has bumps. That it has pain. That it has drawbacks. That there is a game that's being played and there's a team on the field that doesn't want us to win.

Sigh.

That's just a hard one, don't you think? It's one thing to cut familiar teammates... to choose adventure and expect a dragon. But it's another to accept that there are smaller, more sly, more devious and dangerous things in our lives whether we like it or not.

But there's a reason I don't use the "all the world's a stage" setting for your life. It isn't simply a stage. Stages are awesome. They have red felt drapes, floating black floors, and a million cool gadgets to play with. At any time, on a stage, you can just draw the curtains and be nestled in the warm muffled silence.

That's nothing like real life. In life, you have opposition. You do. You can close your eyes, try to block it out, try to stay positive and chant and stand and sing... you can do whatever you want to try to cope with the other side... but it's still there.

It doesn't go away.

The worst thing anyone can ever tell, teach or encourage in another person, in my personal opinion, is the belief that it doesn't exist. To that the negative forces in our lives are just a figment of our imagination. That they are only there by our permission. That we can actually wish or will or positively think them away! How dangerous. How easy it is for you to get tackled.

If you don't believe the other side exists, then you can't and/or won't be prepared for it when it hits you with its next play. And the next. And the next.

I bet you can think of a few parents who, not wanting their kids to ever have to face opposition, go out onto the field and take all the hits for them. That's part of their job in the early years, but it's not their job for their entire lives.

It's our parents' job to teach us, train us and empower us to handle what the opposing team throws at us. Simply taking all the pounding all the time for their child does no one any good. It beats up the parents pretty hard, and leaves the kid unphased. But in the long run, they aren't doing them any favors. They are essentially lying to their kids about the world out there.

What happens when their parents are gone? What happens when their parents get so roughed up and have so many injuries from playing not only their own opposing teams, but their child's as well? Families like this usually have a few other members who are more than happy and willing to take on the job of protecting those new young adults from real life - from any real form of the game, too.

I've seen sisters, aunts and uncles all stepping up to the plate financially, physically or emotionally when the child, who is now a teenager or a young adult, needs more assistance than one set of parents can provide.

But in the end, their son or daughter's opposing team will eventually tackle them. And then what? I'll tell you what - they will *not* be ready for it. They'll be completely unaware. Untrained. Weak. Unwilling. And they will fall.

Fall so easily. I've seen it so many times.

These are young ones who fight the least. They've never seen it, tasted it or even know its name. They don't know what fighting is, never mind know it's an option.

So when the very first member of the opposing team actually gets to touch them - straight on - even with a slight brush of the shoulder - down they go. They give up more quickly or easily than any others I've ever seen. They just wilt in acceptance.

I remember a young man from college who had this exact upbringing. His family hadn't expected anything of him. He was their youngest and their prized possession. He had all the nicest clothes, the nicest cars and the best education. The rest of the family went broke, but they made sure that he was never compromised. He felt no shift in the foundation.

When he finally started to grow up, through the influences of others at his college, it was really hard on him. *Very* hard. He was given an assignment to go on a hike and write in a journal in the middle of it.

Asking us about good hikes, we recommended a favorite trail of ours. Now, keep in mind, we didn't know that he was so sheltered. We didn't know his family had expected so little of him, or had exposed him to so few of the elements. We thought he was a young, strong healthy man.

When he returned he immediately phoned and asked us to come right over. We were so worried. We didn't know what had happened. Had he broken something? Had somebody roughed him up? We knew the hike well so we had a hard time imagining what awful thing could have possibly occurred.

So we ran over to the dorm. We sat down with him. He looked shaken, disturbed and torn. Then we listened...

In short, while crossing a stream, he'd missed a rock and a corner of his shoe became wet. The end.

It took Nick and me a long, long, *long* time to finally understand that this was the huge horror that had occurred.

Like I said, it just takes a brush from the opposing team. His parents, for all their money and for all their sacrifices, had not raised him to be an adult. To be independent. To handle the opposing team. At *all*.

There are other ugly consequences too. Ones we don't always think of, because they tend to be so far apart.

For example, let's take a look at one of my relatives. He grew up in a household where a father was rarely present, but when he was it was a bit touch-and-go. Most of the time he was silent, every once in a while he spoke, but there were times when he would explode. Out of nowhere. Complete silence beforehand... then suddenly a chair would be thrown back and a chest of drawers would be smashed and loud yelling would burst out.

His mother, in these times, simply froze. She did not try to protect the children. She just wanted to be back in his favor. She would look to his father and would weep and her eyes would beg for his mercy, his forgiveness or his acceptance.

As such, this boy grew up with a very large wound in the "startle" part of his wiring. If there was ever a sudden loud yell, sudden anger, or even just a loud noise, he would start shaking and crying. Had his mother comforted him after such loud startles, told him he was safe or even help him calm down afterwards, things would have turned out differently.

But instead he was simply left to feel completely exposed, naked and terrified - completely off center with no way to get back on - whenever he experienced a startling offense, especially from an authority figure.

It was no surprise however, that this proved to be difficult when he took the field on his own. Within his first year out of the house, his boss, albeit a bad one, came into the lab he was working in and shouted at the workers in anger.

My relative immediately wept, right there on the spot, just as his mother had done. He was horrified. He was embarrassed. He had no idea why he was crying and he hated it. He couldn't stop it. He was a wreck.

"Why?" you may ask, "is this so terrible? Are you saying that the downside to ignoring the pain in this world is what? A guy crying in a lab?"

No. I'm not.

Because when this young man had children, he remembered the wound from crying in the lab and said, "I never want them to be like me." And proceeded to commit random scare tactics on his children... out of nowhere.

He'd be playing with them, smiling at them, and then suddenly... out of nowhere... just as he was smiling and they were looking up at him with adoring "daddy eyes," he'd suddenly grit his teeth, scrunch up the angriest face he could think of, and then yell at his kid with a huge and terrible roar.

You can imagine the terror his kids felt. I hate getting their pictures in the mail, because they always have red, tired eyes and puffy faces from a life of instability and inconsistency. They have no idea what "safe" really means.

As I tried to fill my relative in on the damage this behavior was causing, he simply said, "I never want them to go through what I did." Yet here he was, putting them through much, much worse.

And so I say to you, yes, there are bad things in this world. Yes, there is an opposing team. Ignoring it and telling ourselves and our children that it doesn't exist just makes it easier for them to beat us. In fact, it makes it so easy for them, that their opposing teams have the freedom to walk right into their locker room and infiltrate their team. It's much easier to kill us from within.

From the first day that this new dad started roaring at his kids in the middle of play time, then switching right back into a happy face mere seconds later... as his kid stayed still in frozen terror and shock... this dad unknowingly became a key member of his son's opposing team.

I'm sure this dad thought he was a great coach. I know he loves his kids. But he absolutely and firmly believes that his childhood was perfect and that his parents could do no wrong. Even today, his parents are given the highest priority, even over his wife and his kids.

It breaks me in two, just thinking about it.

I too was raised in a home full of avoidance. Thankfully I learned, by the grace of others, about my opposing team and started re-training myself. You heard about my original team. It couldn't handle very much of the real world, but I never would have been able to re-train myself if I hadn't known my enemy.

It's one of the first things I did, when I started over - I adopted "know thine enemy" for myself. Your opposing team has an incredibly high success rate because it knows you, but you don't know them.

The tables have to be turned. We must first admit that there is an opposing team we all face. Then we must admit that it's not just out to get us - but get us good. We must admit it plays dirty, plays rough and has no scruples. And then their own motto of "know thine enemy," must become ours as well.

It's the only way. Ignorance, no matter what they say, isn't bliss. Not when it comes to the game of life. Not even close.

- Common Opposers -

Just as we have many different kinds of teammates, so does our opposing team. Some of them are obvious and come to mind quickly, like financial stressors, but the strongest players, the most lethal ones, are the ones in dark shadow. They move like the wind, unseen, yet powerful.

None of this matters though. Now that you see them - now that they are no longer invisible to you - most of their powers are gone. It's like burglars you know about ahead of time. They can steal a lot if you don't know they are coming. But if you've been alerted to their plans... well, then. They don't have much of a chance, do they?

Of course, our opposing team isn't looking for just a couple of jewels. They are looking to steal all love and life from us. That's much more deadly. Plus, they have centuries of experience. But now you get to actually play them. And you will learn *so* much about them by doing this.

Playing them, standing up to them, tackling them and smashing them - you will learn their scents. You'll start to memorize their plays. You'll start to know what it feels like when they are hitting certain players of yours. You'll get to know how they make you feel and then you'll be able to identify them more quickly.

Let's take the inner critic, for example. Their message is almost always shame. Oh, how the heat of shame does flush my entire body, from head and teeth right down to my toes. My breathe come less easily and I suddenly feel itchy, like I can't be comfortable anywhere, and every single thing around me becomes an object of irritation.

Now, I'm sure this may remind you of many different emotions, and this reaction could truly signal the strike of several different kinds of tactics or plays by the opposing team. But because I've been at this so long, because I've been keeping an eye out and studying them as I play them, I've learned that this reaction, for me, is always completely related to the inner critic.

And so when I feel that terrible flush, I immediately try to run the defensive moves I have learned that work. I use my training and do the following things: I immediately pin the inner critic down and tell it to, well, 'f' off first, and then visually light it on fire.

Then I put on music that makes me want to dance or cheer. This gets me out of my head where the old core training circuitry is firing off. The music drops my energy and focus down and into my body.

I always change the room I am in - I get out of the room where the attack occurred. If I can, I move into open air. The sun, the grass, the sky, the breeze and the leaves and the foliage all tend to pull me right out of my mental spiral. It's a sure fire method for the erasing or re-directing the shame traffic in my brain.

And finally, I usually grab a small piece of dark chocolate. I literally have a stash specifically allocated for these occasions. I don't exactly know how it works (some scientist out there surely knows why), but it has proven to work time and time again on occasions like these.

Of course, not all of these options are available when the inner critic hits, but as you can see, that's led to a number of different defensive plays that I can use no matter where I am.

So let's talk about the common opposers that we all face on the field, whether we know it or not. I could categorize them, as I did with our team members, but today I feel like it's better to literally list them all outright. It's just too important to use shorthand on. If there are any terms you don't understand or that I can't fully explain for you, feel free to us the internet or family doctor to research and learn them. Google them. Wikipedia it.

Remember, I said I stole their playbook. Well these are straight out of it. It's time to "know thine enemy." Dig in and get to know these behaviors, these attacks, these stressors and these blockades. They are the building blocks of your specially designed opposing team. Repeatedly study, research and watch for these the way they watch you and you'll jump leaps and bounds on that golden scoreboard of yours.

Here they are in alphabetical order:

- ✓ Addictions
- ✓ Bad Boundaries
- ✓ Bad Programming
- ✓ Bullies
- ✓ Buttons
- ✓ Codependency
- ✓ The Drama Triangle
- ✓ Emotion Regulation Handicaps
- ✓ Financial
- ✓ The Inner Critic
- ✓ Narcissists
- ✓ Living Underneath a Bad King
- ✓ Physical Abuse
- ✓ Sexual Abuse
- ✓ Spiritual
- ✓ Sides of the Street
- ✓ Startle
- ✓ Sociopaths

Oh what a mess! Right? There's SO many, I know! But don't forget - this is a Top Secret list that only your opposing team has had for nearly your entire life, and having it in your hands now is absolutely the last thing they could ever want.

Now keep in mind that these are just the most common plays. Most of us have at least half of this list to one degree or another on their opposing team's roster, especially in today's culture. The internet has completely unlocked the beast in any and everyone who had one to unlock. We have to be much more prepared today than just a few short years ago.

But here's some good news for you: I have this *entire list* on my opposing team. This is pretty much the exact roster I face everyday when I wake up in the morning... or who greet me in my dreams at night. I know each and all very well.

Yet here I stand. Happy. Healthy. With an amazing marriage with a man who faces one heck of a roster too! But he has one heck of an amazing roster of his own to match it with on the field.

We've learned a lot. We've studying a lot. And we've lived. And have love. Despite all of the odds.

Consider me your success story. There is hope. It *can* be done. You *can* beat your opposing team, and you *can* dominate that scoreboard.

Now, let's take a closer look at a few of those common opposers, shall we?

Bad Programming

This programming, in my opinion, is absolutely your greatest opposition, hands down. It's the least visible of all the players on our opposing teams, and yet they are the tallest, the broadest and the fastest of the entire bunch. These will be the hardest ones to defend against, which is why it's best to train hard and build an amazing offensive line too.

Bad programming occurs during our core training. It's almost impossible to examine it, study it or fight it if some serious work and/or action is not taken to actually *go after* it. It's intense.

For example, a healthy mind and heart, when told the word yes - just that word, alone - yes - will feel a warm glow, a soft hug, a sense of peace or something similar. It's along the lines of something positive. It makes you expand. It makes you smile or feel content.

The word no on the other hand does the exact opposite. It triggers a negative reaction. A slight contraction. A dip of the head.

The word itself is a subtraction. A person will feel uncomfortable or cold.

But an excellent example of bad programming is when a person experiences these emotions in reverse. When a *yes* inspires negativity and contraction, while a *no* makes them feel warm and comfortable - at peace. Can you imagine how this programming plays out in that person's life?

It's would permeate every single moment, corner, memory of their lives. Can you imagine the handicaps they face without even knowing it? The bad decisions about work, people and the communities they join as a result? Programming like this is hard to uncover, and even harder to re-program, but it can be done. And then their opposing team no longer has an automatic touchdown on their hands - the tables have been turned.

Bullies

We all know what a bully is. We mostly hear about them in school settings. But the fact of the matter is that bullying, of all shapes and sizes, is promoted and/or exemplified in almost every piece of western media. If you watch for it, you'll notice how often every joke is made at someone else's expense, or even their own. Every single quirk, characteristic or weakness in anyone or anything is constantly laughed at, poked at, examined and then taken apart.

Then, of course, is there is the incredible increase in ageism. There are constant digs aimed at "old" people. Anyone over 25 is a major target. Even James Bond, only two movies after scoring his 007 rank, is suddenly an "old dog." It's amazing. Bullying is everywhere - celebrated and adored.

Celebrities say they want bullying to stop, but the fact of the matter is that they're just getting started. Start keeping your eyes peeled. Start paying attention to the humor. Listen and analyze and you'll start seeing the incredibly large movement of derision that's training us all to be bullies on some level or another.

Buttons

As one doctorate put it, "our parents install our buttons and then they push them for the rest of our lives." I remember it so clearly. It instantaneously answered a lot of questions for me about so many behaviors I'd seen in others. It of course empowered me as well, to be both more understanding of myself and less worried about taking things personally.

I still remember the first memory that popped into my head when I heard this concept of buttons. I remembered visiting a shop with a client who was checking in on her daughter that worked there. The mother made a comment about one of the items in the store.

Suddenly, without warning, her daughter flew off the handle. I still remember it like yesterday. I hadn't understood how a simple comment could trigger such a reaction. But now the puzzle pieces instantly fell into their place. The mother had pushed a button in her daughter, and her daughter did exactly what she had expected.

It explained why the mother went completely unfazed by the sudden outburst. It also explained why she refused to acknowledge the pain the comment had caused her daughter too. Maybe the mother liked the attention. Maybe she liked exerting her control. Either way, she had clearly installed a button in her daughter, and knew exactly how to push it.

We all have buttons hidden within us. Our parents created them, either knowingly or not. Unfortunately, it's a button anyone can push - like a secret tripwire we didn't know existed - and then a simple comment we make triggers an outburst from our friend, colleague or co-worker.

Women usually take it personally, when in reality, it was just a button installed deep within them.

Emotion Regulation Handicaps

This has a lot to do with our core training. You know how people like to say, "I'm bad at confrontation," or "I'm bad at commitments"? The foundation for those statements lies in how we learned to regulate our emotions during our core training.

What does "regulate" mean? Basically it means how you handle each emotion. For example, if your boss is angry with you, how do you handle it? What about when your parent is mad at you or your spouse, co-worker, etc? Better yet, how do you handle it when you are angry with them? That's emotion regulation.

The first step, in my opinion, is figuring out which emotions there are. I personally love Plutchik's wheel emotions. And I do mean, *love* it! I always say that when you feel overwhelmed or stressed or distracted, you're usually feeling about three different emotions. Then I go and check the wheel and try to identify which are the three I'm feeling, and go from there. You can't face this opposer blind.

The Inner Critic

Let's just say this guy deserves a whole other book. You'll find so many different words for this horrible voice that we all have. It was talked about quite a bit in the 70's and then we just forgot about him. Words that also describe him are the judge, the gremlin or the parent.

It's the voice inside us that tell us certain things, actions, thoughts or behaviors are bad or shameful. Because it's buried so deeply inside us we are rarely aware of it. We do, however, expect everyone to live by the rules of this hidden voice. It's such a deep part of our wiring, that we think it must be the basic voice in all humans.

Unfortunately it's isn't. It's very different for each one of us. And it's probably the most potent and dangerous force within us. I hate it when people say it's something we just have to live with. It's not. It's a cancer. We must go after it with all we have.

People think they can just live with it instead of rooting it out - no. Not if you want a touchdown. No way. We often mistake it for God's voice or our own voice, when really it's someone else's voice entirely that's been passed down from generation to generation and keeps you in physical and emotional bondage. The inner critic will not let you play your full team. It's nothing to laugh at. Ever.

Living Under a Bad King

I've said this so many times before, but the most important lesson I ever learned as a studio owner is that you attract people who are like you. I had a storefront in a strip mall of four units, and the landlord put someone next door who provided the exact same services. I was furious. Until I realized I was nothing like them. We lost one single client to them in our entire stay.

It's the same with bosses, political leaders and peacekeepers. The quality of a principle affects the entire student body of a school. A manager of a branch affects the entire quality of the branch's customer service. A bad political leader leads to bad politics. A bad "king" leads to a bad kingdom. And if you're in that kingdom, it will affect you, one way or another.

It's something to be on the lookout for. I once lived in a city where the police chief changed. He was a brute, rude and caustic. The city immediately felt the shift, because the police force under him started molding to his ways. People who were pulled over suffered emotional tirade from the officers.

The racial profiling increased. The force became brash and inconsistent. It polluted the whole town. Be aware of your atmospheres - whether it be your workplace, county or union. A bad king can change a lot of things.

Narcissists

Let's just say they are another, ahem, growing problem. A recent Harvard study found that narcissism had tripled in colleges in just the last ten years. It's potent and it's harmful. The very first chapter of my very first book was on Narcissism. It's called *The Nissy* and went global the first day I released it. There's a reason for that. It struck a cord. And it's still one of my most well loved and famous pieces to date. (You can catch it in my first book, *Telling the Truth*).

Sociopaths

Sociopaths are dominating the management sectors of the workplace. They easily manipulate others, take the credit for the work of others and present themselves with such arrogance and confidences that people easily believe they earned it, even though they haven't. Their numbers aren't just on the rise, but their lack of ethics or remorse enable them to lie their way to the top without anyone even realizing what they've done to get there.

Learn the signs. Having them in management makes for terrible corporate atmospheres and can eat a company from the inside out before you even notice a single one of their lies. Not only that, but sociopathy seems to be the only type of character Hollywood likes to portray anymore. That's a dangerous web they've been weaving for more than a decade now.

Watching it and living it are two very different things. Know the difference. Spot the behavior. Be ready and be prepared. A sociopath will always play for your opposing team, even if they don't know you. Charm is a verb. It's something that's done to you. Don't ever let it deflect your examination of their real motives.

Spiritual

I don't care how you slice it, but there is the world we see and one we don't. I don't watch paranormal shows or movies, and I don't watch scary ones either - but I remember seeing the Omen as a child - the original one. I don't know why a parent would let very young children see such a movie as that, but they did and... well. I didn't make it through the sleepover. I ended up at home, hiding under my bed.

I've lived a pretty amazing, dense and exciting life up until now, and have seen and experienced more than I could ever put to paper in my lifetime. But I do think, after living so much, that there's a reason that movie freaked me out. There was simply too much truth to it. And I, even as a very young girl, knew it.

I have my own beliefs but I haven never ever asked my readers to accept them or demanded that they agree with them. I believe in your right to think, breathe and live your life free of my, or anyone else's, control or manipulation. Otherwise, this book would not exist.

But I will say this (take it or leave it): evil exists. It does. And in the end, its very bottom line is this: to keep you separate from love. Period.

I believe there are angels and I believe there are demons and I believe there is a constant battle going on around us every single day about that word: love. Demons don't want it in your life. They want your world to be cold, lifeless, bleak, without hope and with nothing but the taste of despair in your mouth every day.

I often think that evil is the head coach of our opposing team. It's probably why this book took so long and I suffered so much pain in order to write it. I think you're worth it though. And that, I can promise you with my hand on a Bible, is because my life is now full and filled with that amazing word: love.

——

And there you have it. Talk about some serious food for thought, right? This is the kind of chapter that will mean different things to you every time you read it. I hope it's done a great job of shedding a lot of light on your own personal opposing team.

Before we move on to hell week, let me just reiterate it once more: your opposing team's strength lies in its ability to know you.

It studies you. It follows you. In order for us to succeed at winning our games, we must do the same with it.

Up until now, most of us never even knew there was a game going on, never mind knowing that we were up against such a big or well-honed team. So take that first big step: admit your opposing team exists. Then see it for what it really is: a beatable team. Once you know them though. And know them *well*.

7 HELL WEEK

Youth, like pristine glass, absorbs the prints of its handlers.

-Mitch Albom

There was a time in the 70's that we as a society uncovered a lot of secrets about how we are molded into the persons we become. That movement continued and eventually it made its way into the mainstream media. We heard people say "my parents did this" or "my parents did that."

By the time we hit the new millennium, we were starting to use terms like "passive-aggressive" and "commitment-phobia" rather regularly. Unfortunately, the new-ness of it has worn off. We may understand ourselves better, and we may even understand those around us better, but we seem to simply stop there.

How many stories I have heard! From women who date men that simply tell them, on the first date, how broken they are. They know themselves quite well. They say they have narcissistic tendencies, or abandonment issues or mommy-issues. But they just say it as if it's an excuse for their behavior.

They don't seek treatment. They don't feel remorse for the pain it causes their date. In fact, they use it more as an excuse. It's as if there's a whole generation of men out there who feel entitled to treat their women badly because, hey - they *did* give them a heads up in the beginning, right?

I cringe when I hear these first date stories told, because the women are usually so impressed by these men. They feel like the men are being vulnerable with them - letting them in... Never stopping for a moment to think why the man *was* so vulnerable with her so soon.

When he cheats on her, vents on her or refuses to commit to her, he always holds the winning card in his back pocket: "but I told you I was this way in the beginning!"

Yup.

What's more disturbing to me, though, is that we, as a culture, are watching the death of compassion. How often I have heard teenagers today fling out the most biting analyses of their parents, their friends - even their teachers and, get this - the celebrities!

Agape I am, as I walk through a beauty store and here some young 13 year old girl rip into whatever artist is playing overhead in the store. They are absolutely ruthless about it. They feel no remorse, no compassion, for pain for others at the wounds they have suffered. They'll attack their vocals, their personal life, their lyrics - as if they were seniors sneering down their noses at the poor little freshman. It's amazing to hear. I can't imagine what they do to those who *aren't* world famous.

The psychology labels have not only grown to become well known, but they have grown to be passé. They aren't an excuse. They are a weakness to be exploited. They are a badge we all must wear and deal with for the rest of our lives.

As such, we've lost the desire to look back and see our roots. We feel like we're "putting the blame" on our parents too much, and we now believe that they all "did the best that they could."

My dears, we are lost if we take this approach... if we minimize the pain or the wounds of our upbringing, simply because they are so common. If we all caught the flu it would be considered an epidemic. But if we are all abused or wounded in childhood, we are normal - not to be healed or attended to.

And we are so scared of the anger of our parents. We are constantly expected to feel only one way about our mothers: thankful. And we are also shoved to feel one way about our fathers: indifferent. "Just forget them," we're told, or "but she's your mother," when you don't call on Mother's Day.

Such refusal to look reality in the eye and act upon it is cultural suicide. We *can* heal and we *can* act upon our wounds - without hate or blame. As one brilliant therapist put it, "we don't blame, we just notice."

It's time for us to "notice" a lot.

———

I love the full quote from Mitch Albom. I believe that in today's society, it will take some bravery on your part to read the following and accept it, just like it was hard to accept that we have an opposing team.

Here is all of what he says:

"All parents damage their children. It cannot be helped. Youth, like pristine glass, absorbs the prints of its handlers. Some parents smudge, others crack, a few shatter childhoods completely into jagged little pieces, beyond repair."

Ah what a quote. I totally agree with all of it... except for one small caveat. No one is beyond repair. At least no one who still has their right mind intact.

And that's you. If you are reading this book, I give you my solemn word that you are not beyond repair. You are probably expecting a catch and yes, there is one. It's this: no one else can save you. Only you can do that.

Oh, it's almost impossible to do on your own, depending on how shattered you are. I don't mean that you won't need others who have been there before to council you, guide you or train you. You will. But at every single step, there is a choice. And it's yours.

How many people I have seen, young people in there early 20's, 30's and 40's, who finally seek help and then... stop midway. They hit a wall they don't want to face. They would rather live with the wounds than go through the pain it takes to heal them.

So no, you are not beyond repair. No matter how smudged, cracked or shattered your glass is. But like most of us, you will have to undergo surgery. The wounds need to be re-opened, the shrapnel removed from the deepest parts of the wound, and then the wound must be fully cleaned before it is stitched up again to finally heal in peace.

Some of us only have one wound. Some of us have many. It can take a year or it can take a lifetime.

But I know a shortcut. I spent a lot of years in therapy and a lot of time on antidepressants until I finally met one therapist who basically did all the work in one single operation. My life turned around in one month. I kid you not. And I haven't been on antidepressants since.

What was the difference? This therapist went after my core training. Hard.

Simply put, he got in my head and re-wired it. Completely. And then I did the homework. It was hard homework, but I have never looked back since.

Was it painful? Yes. Do I wish I'd had it in the beginning? *Heck yes!* Which is why I'm bringing this chapter to you.

- Boot Camp -

Every boot camp has a hell week. This is the week that comes before the normal days of spring training. Oh yes, those training days are tough and hard, but hell week is designed to weed people out.

Literally. Hell week is so hard that it separates the men from the boys, the women from the girls and the strong from the weak. Some say it's designed to test your dedication to the game. Some say it's designed to test your longevity. Some say it's the test of your heart.

Our hell week is no different.

There is a reason people quit therapy.

There is a reason people refuse to go deeper.

There is a reason people would rather ignore the monster in the bedroom than turn and face it.

There's a reason people don't want to take the field, and there's a reason why they like to put others on it instead.

It's hell week. Prepare to be submerged. Prepare to be rewired.

Prepare.

Let's begin.

Core Training

Okay. So remember when I talked about your core training? The training that happened between the ages of 0-4? Well... let's just say that there's a reason I call it core training. Because those are the ages when your body's brain is mapping out its pathways.

Based upon the input your brain receives from your parents, your brain will literally make little freeways in your head connecting all the dots in very specific ways.

For example, when you smile and your parent smiles back, your brain creates a freeway of electricity, using those long little cells called neurons (heck, they even *look* like little freeways!), to go in one specific direction.

In this case, since your smile was matched with a smile, your brain connects the happiness you're feeling to the happiness part of your brain. Basically, in very, very, *very* short terms: your brain learns that when you smile and feel happy, that's a good thing. A positive thing. Something to enjoy. You learn that smiling is the appropriate and positive response to happiness.

You feel safe to do so. You grow up to become an adult that easily smiles when you feel happy.

Now. What if your parent doesn't smile back at you? What if the parent frowns, or gives a look of disgust or exasperation when you smile? That little freeway that your brain maps down does *not* look like the freeway that was mapped when the parent smiled! Oooohhhh no, it sure doesn't.

Instead, the brain maps a different path, so that when you're feeling happy, you will then feel like you are wrong - the freeway is mapped to the shame part of your brain.

I know I'm really simplifying this here, but I bet you're getting the picture. Your brain is one giant system made up of long, long thin cells with connectors on each end - just like freeways with on and off ramps. And your brain, when you see a cupcake in a window for example, will shoot electrons in whatever direction your brain's been mapped to go.

There are several directions those cupcake electrons can go. It just depends on the paths your parents built into you, especially when it comes to "emotion regulation." Depending on your parent, you might feel joy at the sight of the cupcake, disgust at the sight of the cupcake, or sadness at the sight of the cupcake. And that really changes things up, doesn't it? I told you emotions are just as valuable as your other skills!

Now, here are some other ways we see these individual road maps appear in our lives.

I don't have kids yet, but let me tell you! I am white-knuckling it even now at the very thought, before we've even tried to start a family. Why? Because every, and I do mean *every!* Every couple we know talks about they day their first child was born. They all say they felt a change in themselves, in their heads, in their bodies.

As one friend put it, "we both suddenly became two completely different people."

I'm not surprised. We don't remember much about our 0-4 years do we? Some of us have them blocked completely, and that's okay. Your body never allows you to remember something until you finally have the tools to handle it. Trust me. You have teammates that know about them, and they are just hiding them away until you can face and work through them.

Trust your teammates on this subject, friends, especially these ones. Just sayin.'

Now. Even though we don't remember those early years, our brain still has all the mapping that was done during that time. Those roads and freeways were built in certain specific directions, and those roads will *never* go away or change direction unless you have reconstructive surgery on them.

So when we have a child - *BAM!* Oh dear, does that open the flood gates!

Just imagine a whole city in your brain, one that's been abandoned long ago, and sits, for twenty to thirty years doing nothing, growing dusty, but never ever gone. But then suddenly! Whoosh! Baby is here! And wham bam thank you ma'am, the sirens go off in that city and everything suddenly explodes with life.

All the lights suddenly burn bright, the flood lights grow up into the air and yup, you guessed it, the old freeways, the ones that were formed in those core training years, specifically in regards to child rearing, come flooding in.

Honestly, for some of us it's like LA traffic! Lights, horns, honking and beeping at you because hey - you aren't used to these emotions or pathways or ideas or convictions you suddenly have... that you never even knew existed.

And the same darn thing is happening in your spouse.

Let me promise you one thing. If you haven't had your brain re-wired, then I can promise you that a ton of your parenting instincts are going to be solely based upon what you received when you were that age - completely unconsciously of course. Because we wouldn't want all of this to be too easy, right?

And then it usually goes either one of two ways. Either you go with it, because you think your parents were great, okay or just so-so and it's not worth fighting it. *Or* you hated your parents' approach and you can feel it in your body and it scares you. So you hit reverse and try to do the exact opposite. Kind of like my relative who is working hard at startling his son.

Yup. Childbirth. One of the greatest shockers our core training likes to pull on us.

Here's another way, and for me, a more personal one.

I am married to two men. There is the man I fell in love with and said 'yes' to, and then there is the man I ended up being married to. They are two very different men. It's astonishing. And painful.

When I see glimmers of the man I fell in love with, it's like a time warp. I am giddy and giggly and fully flushed with joy and love. I just want to pounce on him and steal his ring and wear it all day. I kid you not.

And then there is the Nick "after marriage." This new Nick took some time for me to finally see and understand clearly. It took a long time to finally see the fully formed "after marriage" Nick since we went through so many huge life stressors in the first five years of our marriage.

But by year six I could tell, especially after all the counseling each of us had been through concerning our extended families, that things had changed. After a couple of heated debates and a great deal of missing hair on my head from the fine art of pulling I'd now developed, Nick finally went to see a counselor to find out what was going on with him.

Once again, the New Life hotline we've learned to use paid off and gave us a great reference - two actually. The first one worked well, but not super well, so Nick called for another reference. He now has a great one and is finally making leaps and strides. It's wonderful!

But before Nick moved on to the second therapist, the first one said something in one of the first sessions that really stuck with me when Nick first shared it. It was as if the therapist took super blurry binoculars away from me and just hit a magic Lasik button. Bam! All was in glorious sharp focus again. Here, in a nutshell, is what he said:

He said that when a person is growing up, they learn and develop all of their social skills and interactions around their families, and therefore they are all the rules that "apply" to family for the rest of that person's life. Think of it as if the coaching positions of every child, until about the ago of 10, is marked "family members only."

The rules, the boundaries, the priorities - everything we learn until we're about 10 or 12 - is purely family based. The "family" rules are drilled right into the core. We learn to play the game their way. All their plays, drills, approaches and attacks are stored in one big huge cabinet. It's full of folder after folder of training materials and plays - "shoulds" and "should-nots." That huge cabinet is called the family cabinet.

Then, when we hit our teenage years, we really separate from our families. We spend less time with them and more time with our peers. Because of that, some peers that we look up to or who seem to influence us more than others, take their place in our coaching section as well. We learn rather quickly that things are different with friends.

The rules are different. Maybe more strict, maybe less. Maybe weird or maybe fun. The point is, another cabinet is moved into our locker room, and that's called the social cabinet.

That's because it's not just folders full of instructions on how to relate to friends. It also fills up with folder regarding work relationships, dating relationships and volunteer/peer relationships, like politics and non-profit work. The point is, the social cabinet sits *next* to the family cabinet. We keep them separate. For a reason.

Haven't you noticed how your friends might change when they are around their families? Or maybe they don't? Maybe you do? Sometimes people aren't allowed to develop relationships outside the family. A social cabinet can be an offense to certain kinds of families and practically labeled a sin, if not worse.

Then, after outlining the two cabinets, the family cabinet and the social cabinet, he talked about what Nick and I were experiencing.

He pointed out that when Nick and I first met, and while we were dating, all of his interactions were based on the allowances laid out in his social cabinet. Socially, he'd learn to be really rather naught and witty and sharp and unfearing. But that's not the Nick his family knows. Both his mother and step-father are "wow" alcoholics, as one of our favorite therapist friends puts it.

They make high-functioning alcoholics look like silly puppets on a string. Needless to say, *that* cabinet, his family cabinet, was... uh... different. Let's just say, the social and the family filing cabinets might have both been in his locker room, but oh... they weren't just on opposite sides of the room... they were different *colors*! One might as well have been hanging from the ceiling, they were so different.

Yeah.

So, as the therapist laid out - our marriage moved my lovely little butt and its folder right up and out of the social cabinet and splat. Right into the family one. Crap. I was doomed from the start. It explained so much.

You have to understand. Nick just *didn't* have a mother. The abuse was horrific. He was abandoned, left alone in scary places... I can hardly write about it. Nor can I in regards to his father either. I'd seen a lot before I met Nick. I'd worked in some of the scariest neighborhoods in America. But even so, his life shocked me.

In short, my husband wasn't just hurt by his parents. He wasn't just abused. He was *destroyed*.

And here I was, older, wiser, having already done so much work. I was the mediator of my family - the one who calmed the storm and made everything okay. So it's no surprise that so many of Nick's teammates see my strength and just want to nuzzle and cuddle right up to it, to nip and suckle at the warmth that was denied him at every single start.

But those patterns trigger my own abuse and the ball rolls down the hill... the wounds reopen and our lives begin to bleed. Marriages can heal or they can harm. It is up to both Nick and I, every day, to make the choices that heal us. If we are two whole teams, our love can light up the darkest midnight sky.

If even one of us chooses to steal another's teammate for our own comfort, relief or gain - it weakens both teams. We waiver. We fall. It's a pattern not easily broken, but broken it can be.

It's amazing how far we have come. We are amazing humans, are we not? With the most incredible ability to heal from the more terrible of circumstances.

I am so deeply and humbly grateful for the help Nick and I have both found. We both knew when it was time to call in a new coach to help us re-train our inner workings and instincts. We were blessed enough to dig hard and finally find the right ones.

Who would he and I be, without the teammates each of us were awarded with - who now fight - despite the despairs of their captains? I know Who gave us those teammates, we know Who provided the right coaches in our times of need and if I've ever, *ever!* been more grateful... then this is it - this moment right now.

Does it suck that I'm suddenly being treated like a mom instead of wife... no, let me clarify... *his* mom, instead of a wife? Of course. Those wounds go deep. I get handed his rages, the thrown chairs, the weeping and the crawling... and my blood does run.

Just believe me when I say, core training is everything. I was the baby whose parents grimaced when I smiled. When someone tells me no, I feel safe. When someone tells me yes, I feel terrified. Imagine living with that little mess of a woman. Marriage is a miracle. Ours is no exception.

Core training isn't a joke. It's for life. Here's one last example for you.

The Love Map. I'm sure you've heard of it, if you love the terms neurons and wiring as much as I do. Maybe you've heard different versions of it, like the common sayings that women marry someone like their father, or men marry someone like their mothers. If you haven't heard the term "love map" before, I'm sure you've heard some of its claims somewhere at some point.

The basic gist of it is that yes, just as I described the freeways your parents build into your brain, so do they develop and create your "love map." The only difference here is that the Love Map theory focuses on how you feel, process and experience love - any kind of love. It makes sense.

I once heard a story of a boy who was, while visiting his father on the weekends, fed nothing but big tubs of Cool Whip. The dad, years later, proclaimed, "Oh yes! I did that because it always made him smile." And so, to this day, the boy turned man feels loved by eating a tub of Cool Whip.

If a mother goes through a million marriages, a daughter has a hard time trusting a man. If a father thinks women are promiscuous and evil, then so does the son.

What's interesting to me is that, at least from all the evidence I've seen, recorded and gathered throughout the years, the negative aspects of said Love Maps, etc. seem to teeter totter while a person is in there 20's and 30's.

It's as if they are somewhat unsure of whether or not to go with the social cabinet or the family cabinet.

After all, a person has just spent their most recent years with their social cabinet, and their influence and the person's freedom from time with their family (assuming the two are very dissimilar) makes it seem and feel easy to continue differentiating. But I feel like I always see this kind of kick that happens.

I've seen it in 27 year olds and I've seen it in 38 year olds... there's this sudden change in the person - like they finally realize that they have a choice to make. They've finally seen that the world is huge, hard and that to continue individuating is to take more risks.

These days, I feel like no one takes risks anymore. The family cabinet is winning out all over the place. They let it rule them... call them back to "what they know,"... whether by actually moving back to the town where they grew up, or even into the house where they grew up, or having a family of their own before they are really ready for one.

I get it. I understand this 'kick.'

Right now, I'm watching a lot of my own friends go through it. I've seen the looks in their eyes and I feel the same things reflected in my own soul. So I sat and thought about it. It gnawed at me for a bit. And then it came to me. Ironically, it happened when I was taking down lights from a big tree that we'd had white lights on.

We had circled the trunk with them, and then found ourselves in a bit of a tangle trying to get them around all of the large and sprawling trunks and branches, and smaller branches... it went on and on. Then suddenly I saw it dawned on me.

A friend of ours was in a particularly dark place and was really struggling to get out of it. As I held onto one of the smaller trunks, I saw him there, sitting on the branch. You see, they suddenly symbolized the choices that we make in life. The trunk is our childhood, our Training Season, our roots the core training, etc.

But each branch symbolized a decision we had made in adulthood. And that was it. Once you chose a branch, you were *on* that branch.

Oh, it also branched out into other smaller branches, giving him a left or a right turn, but I felt as if he knew he'd chosen himself into a corner - there weren't many more major life decisions to be made. Not too many plays left in his book. His favorite teammates had been used, but he had left much too many on the bench.

And I could just feel him, sitting on the branch where my hand was, looking over at the other branch, the one with all the big hearty long leaves that didn't start for a long, long time, leaving plenty of trunk and choices to still travel. God, I could hear him bouncing his branch. I felt him - yearning in agony to jump branches.

I could almost taste his need, his desire to go backwards. To move back towards the trunk of the tree where so many branches/options used to be. But he'd gone too far. Going back wasn't possible. He was almost to the very edge of his last branch - where he only had a few twigs to choose from.

He'd played himself into a corner.

For him his "future" is actually here. It's arrived. Suddenly old age and over-the-hill don't seem nearly as far off as they used to be.

Maybe this is what you would call a mid-life crisis - but his is happening much younger, and we can just tell - there's no way a fancy race car or a new motorcycle is going to satisfy any of his kind of panic pains.

I worry that he'll make the decision I've seen so many other couples or friends make.

They go on back to their old ways, their safe ways... to the re-used broken down freeways that have been used and used and used - over and over again. They move back to the city they were raised in. They start calling their mother a lot, or they start acting like they're single and in college again. They drink, drink, drink and watch the game and play Grand Theft Auto or get serious with their local wine club.

Or he could make some of the hard decisions and... Start over again. Much more difficult, much more courageous and a much more probable outlook for that jump he's dying to make to another younger, lengthy branch.

We will see.

I've noticed something else. I've noticed that those who have chosen to stay with unhealthy patterns, because they were able to hide them or control them and keep their ugliness & consequences under the rug during the first half of their life, aren't able to keep the ugly from showing when they get older. It's like watching a ball of yarn on their sweater.

Someone starts pulling it at around 50-65, depending on how bad the damage is, and it just keeps unraveling until they are stark naked. And we all get to see it. The rage. The racism. The judgment. The cruelty. It all increases, unravels and spins marvelously out of control and sprays everyone in the contact zone.

You don't see it much in those who had a healthy happy childhood really, or who made the hard decisions and married who they loved, not who they were told to love, by either their family or even their mate. Nor do you see it in those who moved away and made their own start for themselves, a new life, a new family and their lives are full of joy, dance and hope - because what they have and what they've learned will continue on in their children's children.

Our core training. Ages 0-4. Learn it. Know it. And for heaven's sake, if your baby smiles at you, do me the lovely wee favor of smiling back? Thanks.

- The Rewire -

The wonderful news is that we don't have to live and die by our cabinets. We don't have to live by either our Family rules or our Social rules. We can start all over again.

I believe we never know who we truly are, especially those of us who were either molded or neglected, until we are free to roam our locker rooms. But we're never free to do that unless we take all that core training that fights us every step of the way - and remove it. Delete it. Reboot our brains. Wipe the memory. Undo the chains, the freeways and the neural pathways.

So here we are. The hardest part of hell week. Where it all happens.

It's the part where we take a bulldozer and raze the neural pathways in our brain. Or in other words, it's the part where we tear down the cities and freeways our core training built into our brain to make way for the new cities - the healthy cities - the ones that make us grow as we get older instead of contract as we get older..

Make no mistake. These freeways aren't dirt roads. They aren't even a black layer of pavement. No, these freeways tore deep into the foundation of your mind and soul, knocked reinforced steel deep down and built layer upon layer of rock, cement and cast iron rods to make wide, long range and earthquake proof freeways, highways and interstate paths along the entire map of your brain.

My years upon years of therapy helped me avoid certain freeways when I was in a good place or on certain anti-depressants. I had amazing therapists who did amazing work. They, along with some other amazing people in my life, recommended some extremely powerful books for me.

So I'm going to share with you a few of those that were the

77

most pivotal for me. And then, when I'm done sharing about those, I'm going to tell you about what I did to permanently damage my core training. It gave me a new start at life. It will be quite the ride!

Let's do it.

Boundaries

The first book to make a huge impact on my life for the better was Cloud & Townsend's *Boundaries*. Yes, it's a faith book, but it doesn't read like one. They are at the edge of the church communities, and there are a great many churches that find their approaches too radical.

In my book, that means their approaches actually work. I'm not a "lipstick on a pig" kind of girl. I tried smiling through all of my bad wiring, and it got my in a hospital less than one year into my adult life.

Lipstick on a pig, indeed. This ain't that kinda book.

So yes, *Boundaries* dramatically changed my life. In fact, this book was my very first pivot point. Had I not found it, I don't think I would have learned anything else I've talked about in this book. Yes. It was that important in my journey.

I didn't know it, but I had the worst boundaries in the history of the world. And sadly, but not surprisingly, after I'd read the book, made my notes and then proceeded to make the changes in my life accordingly, I had to change into new communities. I had to make new friends and new acquaintances once I had laid down new and healthier boundaries.

You see, if you have unhealthy behaviors, then you will attract unhealthy people with "matching" behaviors. For example, I was a high functioning girl, who could handle about twelve million things at once if I was asked to.

It didn't matter if it was in my job description or not - if you asked me to do something for you, I'd say yes. This worked out extremely well for some of the youth pastors at the church I was working in. They piled nearly all of their entire workloads upon me, while they went for bike rides, dates and the couch to read a myriad of books. I remember the U2 biography rather well.

I never thought anything about it. Until I couldn't do it all anymore. Until I crashed. Like a computer whose circuits become overloaded, I melted.

And in the melting, came the truth.

They didn't want me any other way.

They didn't know how to survive without the "old" me who did triple the amount of work I was supposed to. They didn't know how to handle or complete their jobs on their own. They didn't know how to function when I was away sick, and they most *certainly* didn't know how to listen to my own new "no" when I came back to work.

I couldn't live through another meltdown again, so the "new" me had to turn down half of the work they had previously put on my plate. Things, may I just say, did *not* go well. Finally, I had to quit. I moved to another church. I started over.

It worked. People met me, the girl with new boundaries, and they didn't ask for more - because now I was attracted to people with healthier boundaries - not like before. I could spot those men, women and pastors, who loved leaning their lives upon another person's back.

I stayed far, far away from them. Needless to say, I had to start over with friends too. I couldn't *believe* how many of my 'friends' didn't show up to the hospital when I had that meltdown! They were no where to be found. My roommate showed. Her friends came with her. They were wonderful.

But the people I had chosen to be my close friends... they never came.

One finally did, and I'll never forget it - I even wrote an extremely painful poem about it. She walked in, and sat next to my bed. She then looked down at me, finally, but her face was filled with such shame and disgust that I will never forget it. Ever. "What kind of witness is this, Katherine?" she asked.

Lipstick on a pig. She didn't like my wounds showing. It didn't show the world that being "saved" saved you from *everything*.

Ah, my dear girl. She didn't know just how clearly the world saw us. It was our final day as friends. It was hard. I don't regret it.

The only issue I have with the book *Boundaries* is that it isn't quite upfront about how people will react to you once you put new ones in place. I think their book *Safe People* is *much*, much more honest about that. But I would never have made it out of the hospital without *Boundaries*.

Bottom line? *Boundaries* changed my life. So did two of their other books: *Safe People* and *12 "Christian" Beliefs That Can Drive You*

Crazy (no kidding!). I may have been a literature major, but I never even remotely came close to highlighting any textbook or manual or manuscript at UCLA like I highlighted these puppies.

They changed my life.

Feeling Good

So did *Feeling Good*. The big guns will use the big words and, hold on to your hats here! They will tell you it's the best book on cognitive-behavioral therapy. Whew. What a mouthful!

Whatever. I'm not a psychologist and I'm not a doctorate either. I'm just the girl that was beaten to the tiniest pulp of a membrane through a very long bevy of physical, sexual and mental abuse and trauma.

And, I might add, I'm the girl who was literally removed from any and all of the teachers who said I was gifted or who said I could write, and had it screwed into my brain in every way shape and form that writing was a sin - an ugly thing that only homeless people do.

And yet here I am. Booyah. *Feeling Good* played a huge part.

So let me put it in our "normal" human-speak, shall I? *Feeling Good* is an extremely well written and accessible book that breaks down ways to rewire our brain. First it helps you uncover and expose all lot of the wiring you have, and second, it helps you fight back.

Like I said, the big words are cognitive therapy, but really it's just becoming aware of the Inner Critic, one of the big guys on your opposing team that I listed for you in *Chapter 6: Your Opposition*.

You have to be willing to pick up a paper and pen at times, but like I said, the choice for you to get better is, and will always be, in your own hands. *Feeling Good* is an incredible tool, but only if you choose to use it.

Something to note is that *Feeling Good* is about six or seven different books in one. The reason that it keeps taking the #1 spot every year for the book most recommended by psychologists, counselors and family therapists is because the many chapters address a myriad of queries - and they address them *well*. It's one of the best written books out there...

For example, the updated *Feeling Good Handbook* has a chapter on good communication. That chapter could stand alone! Easily.

And then there's the chapter on how to measure your level of depression - are you going through a normal episode of the blues? Or are you experiencing Major Depression, a much more serious kind of depression.

In short, the book goes after more than one city of freeways in your brain. I personally like the fallacies - the patterns I get into, like minimizing the positive and maximizing the negative. Those habits alone had me losing sleep over one single student in a class of 40.

I would have completely missed all of the successes I had in the classroom as a teacher and would have only seen the failures. Shortly after I left the field of teaching, I found out that I was known as the best teacher in the district in my subject. Had I not discovered this poor programming in my head through *Feeling Good*, I would not have believed the superintendent who shared this with me.

If you don't do books, get the audio version. If it's overwhelming, stick to reading and re-reading one chapter at a time. The entire book is designed to combat and rewire your core training. Very few people have the power to help you do this, never mind do it in writing. The book is a gift, in my opinion.

It's less than a trip to a doctor, and it will pay off big time in the long run. Or you can skip it and go straight to the money spot: ACT.

ACT

Know from whence you came.
If you know whence you came, there are absolutely no
limitations to where you can go.
- James Baldwin

Welcome to the big show. Affect Centered Therapy.

Again, I will put it in words we mere mortals can understand, but I do think it's worth knowing the actual word-y term as well. This is because ACT is a rather new therapy. Very few people are trained in it. I suspect, however, that once it takes off... wow. It will start a revolution.

But I think there will be a lot of therapists that will resist it, sadly. And for the worst reason possible. Why? Because it's the biggest shortcut in therapy I've ever seen. This is going to sound like a sales pitch, but please - please don't take it that way.

It's just that I'd been in and out of therapy for almost 15 years, and for half of those I was on at least one or more antidepressants. In nine hours of ACT, I was off of the medication and happier than I've ever been. I've grown up, I'm stronger and I now have a team the plays pretty darn well, thank you.

But I don't think of ACT as a way to get off medication, though. I don't think it does that for everyone, and it certainly wasn't what sold me on doing ACT. I had simply hit a wall that even my extremely talented therapist couldn't help me climb. So he recommended me to someone else.

He even came with me, along with my husband, for the first session. To this day, I am extremely grateful. I needed it. I was in really, really, *really* bad shape. It's very unusual and most won't do such a thing, but it helped me trust what was going on in that first session. Thank goodness I did!

(No matter what profession you are in, by the way, it's always a sign of character and truth and health when someone admits they can do no more, or are out of their league or are in an area they don't know as well and... actually recommends someone else. It's rare now, and a healthy hearty practice.)

So let me break ACT down for you, because it's not your average therapy session. Not even close. My first few sessions were three hours each. It never felt like it though.

I've had so many doctors lean in when I tell them about my experiences with ACT, but I want you to be able to lean in too. I want you to understand exactly what it did to my wiring. Let's see if I can...

ACT's entire foundation is based on the premise that our injurious behaviors come from wiring that occurs during our core training. Things like impulsive eating, drug addiction, reliving sexual abuse and even narcissism are all targets ACT was developed for, though it can tackle just about anything, from noise therapy, to codependency problems to trust issues.

In order to focus in on the wiring that's faulty, you're walked through each of the basic emotions we have and see exactly how our body handles those emotions. The big word for this is emotion regulation.

The real-speak is: hey - when you're scared on a level 3 on a chart of ten - do your knees tense upwards? Or does your whole body shake? Does your neck start to hurt? Your chest? Or do you not feel anything at all?

Then, in a very gentle walkthrough of all of this, we move on to another emotion. Very quickly (okay, not so quickly, but you understand what I'm saying), you go through each of the emotions and you find out which ones have really faulty wiring.

For example, when my therapist started moving into the emotion called yearning - well. I didn't even know what that was! He gave me three different examples and no, nope and nada - couldn't feel or pinpoint anything at all in me except, "what the heck is he talking about? There's no such thing, right?"

So, bingo. My poor yearning teammate was chained up and stuffed in the last row of the locker room. Good to know!

Then come the others - anger, fear, joy, hope... on and on. It's as if they are mapping your brain, learning where the freeways are, where they are not and whether they are harmful or helpful.

Then, in short, once all the wiring is uncovered - the rewiring begins. Step by step, emotion by emotion, fear by fear, all at the pace you need to go. It's gentle, it's deep and it's very vulnerable, but it's nothing like talking with a therapist or sharing/swapping stories.

In some ways, I shared a mere morsel of the things I'd shared with other doctors, but I think what was shared were those memories at the very roots of my tree, not the leaves. Then, step by step, as I made choice after choice to continue on, those wounds were cleaned out, sewn up and bandaged - and the healing finally - finally! - really began.

Since our ACT therapist was more than two hours away from our home, we learned to book a hotel room near his office and go there to rest after each three hour session. I'd lie on the bed, close my eyes, and let my mind's little electric synapses get used to traveling the new freeways that had been built- testing them out, learning to trust them.

I could feel them run, and run and run - in places I could tell were unused - places that were very new for me and my body. Sometimes I slept. And always, for some unknown reason, we stopped by the See's Candy Shop and bought a single piece of chocolate for each of us.

My life never was the same after that. People who knew me from before noticed a significant change in me. They saw the newfound joy, the new laughter and mostly, the new confidence. I took care of myself better, understood my triggers a whole lot more, and when I could, I would read up on the books that he would reference or recommend.

That hasn't changed. It's been years now. And I've only done one thing since then: I've grown up. I started by make the "hardest cut." That did a whole lot of the work right there. There were a lot of things that fell into place with that one move.

Letting go of my abusers, before I even knew they were abusers, was probably one of my biggest choices of all. During the process I was also given the strength, knowledge and insight I needed to start over and began living with some kind of a clean slate, if you will.

I had been introduced to my stadium. I saw the field and who was on my team. I started taking other people's teammates off my team, and finally put them elsewhere. I was introduced to my locker room and after a while, not only began to see it clearly, but was able to start meeting my teammates that I hadn't known existed.

As time past, I started strengthening my teammates that I had always had, weak as they might have been. The more I took care of my teammates, the more teammates I discovered.

Sometimes they just appeared - something in life triggered them and freed them. Like writing. There was a turning point in the community I had been invested in during that period of my life. It was heartbreaking and it was frustrating and so I wrote something out of sheer frustration.

Then it took off. It boomed. But that wasn't enough for me to realize Writing was a teammate of mine. You know what it took? A college student.

I'll never forget it. He was working as support staff for an event I'd been contracted for. Since it was in the same community I had written my now-famous piece, *The Nissy*, he had read it.

I didn't know him, but he turned to me in the lunchroom one day and introduced himself. He told me that he'd really enjoyed my article and had read it several times. As we discussed it, he clearly became aware that I didn't realize how special it was that he'd read it, even though we didn't know each other.

Finally he just said, "I would do *anything* to get someone to read what I've written." Then he proceeded to list all that he'd written, for our community and for his classes and professors, etc.

I just stood there, frozen. You see, I couldn't relate to his experience at all. People had always loved my writing. As he listed his pieces, professor after professor, teacher after teacher, TA after TA appeared before me... all the times they hugged my papers before handing them back. Or handing them back without a single note but an A+, shaking their heads saying they couldn't find fault with anything...

...and perhaps most of all... the day my favorite and most esteemed head of the Literature department left a note on one of my notebooks I'd turned in... "You should keep this for your children and your grandchildren to read." My TA even made a point of stating that he'd worked with the man for five years, and he had never seen him make such a statement to anyone.

And I had thought that was a bad thing. Oh, core training...

So I simply can't emphasize how stunned I was at this young man's words, and the puzzle pieces he was putting into place. As this college student talked, I was introduced into the real world. Others didn't have these experiences? People write things that others refuse to read???

You probably think I'm crazy as I say this. Years later I can truly see your point. But please understand... when your core training teaches you that writing is easy, poor, something to be ashamed of, you never notice it. Your body learns to overlook it.

When you are wired to think you have nothing to offer this world outside of the fields that have been chosen for you, well - let's just say my world split in two that day.

I'd like to say that was the day - no - the exact moment- when I met my teammate Writing. I'm so grateful for that college student. I don't even know his name.

Over the following weeks and months I continued to write, this time understanding that I might just be different than others in this area - that it just might be what I was meant to do in life. The longer that thought prevailed within me, the more memories came back to me.

Memory after memory after memory of the awards, of the praise, of the pushes by teachers and counselors and the like who told my parents I was different. I was gifted in the area of writing. One teacher, I finally remembered, actually came to the house to visit my parents and tell them how amazing I was at a writing competition (see! I *still* didn't pick up on it!).

I remember my dad closing the door on him, bothered by the intrusion. I remember everything he was wearing on that day - from his socks to the sweatband on his head. That tells you a lot right there - my detailed memory.

(I've since learned what a big flag that is - when our bodies retain detailed memories from our core training years. Today I like to journal about them when I remember them - I learn more about myself and it helps me to heal the wounds from those days.)

So. My story about this college student is simply to tell you how I met Writing, one of my strongest and most natural teammates. It was exciting. It was brave! It was wonderful. It was... scandalous. Scandalous! Very scandalous indeed for me. But I loved it. I loved meeting Writing. I love learning about her.

Meeting Writing was so revealing and empowering that I started searching the other lockers too, looking for teammates my core training had locked up or silenced somewhere. Still, I mostly meet them when I'm not looking for them. It often happens when someone or something, like this run-in with Mr. College Guy, sparks an awakening - a realization in me.

I hate to be cliché, but meeting teammates really does feel like a light bulb going on! There's just more light in the room, no two ways about it. So light bulb after light bulb my team grew, expanded and strengthened. I learned how to process them. I learned how to train them for the field, and play them at their best.

Five years later and I'm still discovering teammates. I have a pretty full team by now, and I really love every single part of them. It feels good to use them and I feel strong in my ability to outwit, outplay and outrun my opposing team. So many of my hard decisions are behind me.

When you make your very first hard decision... it's just that: incredibly hard. When you make a second one - wow, it's still incredibly hard. But I'm on hard decision number 157 by now and I have to say... the game is getting to be fun. Life is exciting. The game is exciting. It's an adventure and I love it and I grow all the time. I'm in love with life.

That's what we were made for, right? To live it up and to live it down. And never forget, by the way - if the opposing team's goal is to keep you as far as possible from the word Love, then can you imagine your life when you're winning it? Love, love, love, love. In spades.

Yes, hard knocks do come, but my opposing team rarely scores anymore. After a life of losing, it feels good. It feels amazing. And I look back, and I mourn the days I couldn't make a single touchdown - the days I didn't know who my teammates were, what they could do or how many were locked up tight in the basement of my locker room.

It's been work and it's been hard, but oh! How I have been repaid in full for it! Oh! The joy that is my life now, and how amazing it is to watch myself do things that I was too afraid to do even months ago.

This is my life. My cup overflows. There is hope for those whose glass has been shattered.

———

But in all of this victory over my core training - the impossible actually becoming possible - there was one sad theme that still recurs even today. I look back at all my amazing therapists who came before, and I would remember things that they had said, or looks they had made when I mentioned certain people in my life.

I quietly started putting the pieces together - they had *known* it was my core training after all. They had *known* who my abusers were and they never, ever, *ever!* told me!

I don't know if they thought I couldn't handle it. In the case of a few of them, I absolutely know that they thought I'd already figured it out. But I *hadn't*. But I wanted to. I *needed* things spelled out for me - I thirsted for it. Some therapists, no, most therapists, keep their clients dependent on them, I know, but...

Recently I was referred to an "amazing" therapist that friends had raved about. Holy cow. I have never met such a controlling, negative or demanding therapist in my life. My freedom drove her nuts. I'd heard of therapists like her, but hadn't met one yet.

Wow. It's a well known fact that children who had little or no power in their childhood or were emotionally abused in their childhood, become therapists in order to finally have power over someone else for a change. But that makes the client dependent upon them.

ACT does the exact opposite. I don't think any of my therapists ever wanted me to be dependent upon them, but I know now that they saw exactly how messed up I was, and never thought to let me in on that secret.

I wanted to know. I needed to know. I hate the fact that I spent so many years on the couch or on antidepressants doing things that put little band aids on much deeper wounds.

But then again, I'm different. I'm the one who says, "Yes. It's worth it." And I make the choice to move forward. I make the hard decisions, not the easy ones. Like I said, the choice is in *your* hands. I suspect my therapists thought I was like most people, who want to sweep up after the monster instead of face it.

I, for one, wanted a sword to fight with. I wanted to see the landscape before me clearly, as I hoped the therapist did. But I felt like I was blindfolded, and I was there, sitting in their offices, asking- waiting - *begging* - for the blindfold to be removed from my eyes.

I wanted to see that monster and slay it. ACT does exactly that. It's not for the faint of heart, but it *is* the cup of life for the brave.

———

Before we move on to the "after party" of hell week, spring training, I'd like to share a story with you of someone who did not make the hard choices. She did not make the hard decisions.

She made some soft decisions. She made some round-about patches over little holes here and little holes there in her team - band-aids really - but she swerved away when her therapist tried to take her own blindfold off and show her the monster in her landscape.

In the end, it took her soul away. In the end, she could no longer face her friends, even. In the end she lost all of them, except for the monster. That alone is who she is left with.

It was her choice.

With every step.

And we have lost her... to the wind.

I mourn for her heart every day. Or maybe I should say I mourn for the death of this woman, and who she once was. Because the darker our demons are, the more likely we are to become them. The less we try to separate from those who hurt us, the more we are destined to hurt others.

It is the tangled web of heat and desire - of blood and of bone - that yanks us down into the dark dank history of family.

TOUCHDOWN

Let me tell you something. Family is not all that they say it is. You're right: we can't choose our family. You're wrong: we don't have to inherit their sins.

I visited a family member recently who is estranged from the entire clan. One of my parents came from a rather large family full of children who all now live amazingly close to one another, who always take vacations together, who always mix their money and who sadly, place their families lower than their own.

Cancer? They tell each other, not their families. Near death? They tell each other, not their families. Accident? They tell each other, not their families.

But there is one they never speak of. I remembered him as a child. We'd seen him only once or twice growing up and I remembered how incredibly charismatic and funny he was. He made me laugh, and I didn't laugh all that much with family.

But then we never heard from him again. When I was married, the family refused to give me his address. They never told me what was wrong. They never told me why they'd separated from him. The most I ever learned was that he had received an electric shock treatment once - and that was because of a medical family history question.

I realized - on the day I learned such a scary thing - that I would have probably gone to the grave without knowing such a thing had happened to our kin. How startled I was, confused and baffled, to learn such a terrible thing just out of the blue. Why?

That push coughed up a, "we split over religious differences." Nothing about the past. And a lie about the present.

Ah, family secrets. How devastating they can be. But when you get to peek into their box and learn a few of them... oh, how much they do tell!

And then, suddenly, as if by fate, my husband and I found ourselves in the little rickety town where he lived - in the house the whole family had grown up in. I knew the name of the town had sounded familiar and when I realized where we were - I quickly texted my family for the address.

And they gave it without hesitation. There was no warning. Family secrets. Some should never be secret.

It was a short visit. We didn't stay long. But we stayed longer than we should have.

On Day 1 we had a lot of fun. He showed us around town. We

89

traded traveling stories. He showed us newspaper articles and papers he'd written. It was wonderful meeting another traveler in the family.

Then later at night, we heard about family. And we saw the rest of the house. We learned that when he came home with his first paycheck as a doctor and showed his father, his father replied with spit. He looked his son in the eye, grit his teeth with disgust and spat out, "And you never even got your hands dirty."

We learned all the things my relative did with his life afterwards to try to win back that man's approval. He biked across the United States, hitting every place his father had ever worked. He even had a sign on his wall: Obey Father & Mother.

It was in all caps. All black. Hand pressed black bold letters on hard white cardboard... the letters blazed more than six inches tall. OBEY FATHER. OBEY MOTHER.

If you think that's odd, or a bit scary, or something out of a creepy movie... you'd be right.

On Day 2 he seemed different. Unsettled. The later in the day it grew, the more he warned us about strange things. Like driving. He said we shouldn't drive our car anymore - it was too dangerous. Bikes were the only safe thing for traveling.

He grew angry while telling us stories. Not all the time, but it was enough. It reminded me of the rages I'd seen in his other family members. Then we learned more about family. Much more.

We learned he had received 43 electric shock treatments, not one. We learned how sick he was and for how long - oh, how *long!* he had been in that hospital. And we learned that while he was there, the hospital advertised a large seminar for the family members of patients to help them understand and cope with what was going on...

No one from his family came. No one. Though they were a large family. And all lived nearby.

This was hard to hear, learn, take in - everything. My brain was swirling as we walked away from that house for the rest of the night.

It was hard because my own family had done the same when I was sick. Hard, because I saw my own pain reflected in his own eyes. Hard because I saw his shame and it mirrored my own. Hard because I understood him *so* well. Hard because I now saw what my family wanted me to be - expected me to be - desired me to be.

My life scrolled itself across my mind, and all the blanks stood. Now filled.

The only difference between him and I were the number of years on this earth. I turned to Nick as we walked away that day, "This was my future. This would have been me. I am him. All of him."

I thought I had deserved it. I thought I had earned it. I thought I was special in my ugliness and depravity. But I was not alone. I was the inheritance of my family. In flesh.

And on Day 3, as we watched his unraveling become complete, he held us at knife point.

Oh, the secrets of family. Oh, how much they tell us. And oh, the web that is our core training... the obedience that we must serve.

I cannot tell you how much I learned in those few short hours and days with him, in the house my father grew up in, in the home where my deepest roots lie. I cannot even begin to tell you...

But I can tell you this. This woman I have mentioned, the friend that constantly told my husband and I, "See, you *can't* go against family. You *can't*. That is *not* an option." She was wrong. She stayed. And now she has been breaking the law, literally, and falling down a ladder into the dangerous world that her wildly insane mother does live. She has made her bed. She will lie in a tomb with her "family."

I refuse.

I refuse to do so. I will not be their flesh.

There is a wonderful piece of verse in the scriptures that gave me hope as a young teenager, even when I didn't know what it really meant, especially in terms of me and my own family. It simply said, in one line, that He can, and will, break us out of our blood line should we choose to do so.

I think all of my locked up teammates in my locker room were all beating the doors, rattling their cages, just trying to get my attention when I read it. All I remember is that, in reading it, it made my shoulders suddenly drop in relief. It was a promise that I reached out and grabbed, the thorns of it piercing my hand. I held it firmly, like a thief holds his precious diamond.

I often wonder about the story of Jesus, asking a would-be follower to follow him immediately.

The man said "Sure. Just let me get things tied up with my

family." And Jesus said no. I wonder about that story a lot these days.

I cannot tell you how many people have told me, when they are presented with the option of new freedom, new life and air, "but my family..." One even told me, "but my cat..." Ah. The choices.

But even so, here is that verse's promise: we can cut the cord and float up out of the deep dark and vast ocean of pressure... and we can come crashing into daylight... spluttering up into the golden sun and air with a sea of diamond lights sparkling from one amazing horizon to the other.

It promises that no matter how thick, deep and long that cord is, we can be free of it. We can meet the sun.

We can...

If we cut the cord. The cord that is family.

8 SPRING TRAINING

Hell week is over and the hardest part of this entire book is most likely over for you too. Self examination is not always easy, but it can be enlightening and exciting - once you get used to it. The benefits outweigh the cost by a million miles.

Now it's time to move on to the bulk of the training that you can use in your everyday lives right now. Let's get your team into shape.

> The wise coach develops not only the fullest physical potential
> in his charges, but also those capacities and habits of mind and
> body which will enrich and ennoble their later years.
> *Geoffrey Dyson*

Just as football teams do, we need in both offense and defense. There's so much we can do when it comes to training for each. There are specific tactics for offense, just as there are for defense. Luckily, in life, there are some tactics that overlap between the two. So the stronger we become in one line of defense, the strong we become in another line of offense.

It's really easy to know which one we need, though. We definitely know when we are on the offense and when we are on the defense. Life is very much like a football game in that way, isn't it?

Sometimes we feel like we're gaining ground fast - moving

forward easily and catching all the right plays in all the right moments. And then - whip! The tables turn and suddenly life is pushing right back. Your opposing team makes some extremely strong plays out of nowhere and suddenly you can't get a single touchdown in there.

Then there are they days when you are making steady progress forward. Down after down you move the ball, closer and closer to the end zone. We can go for months, years even, like this - plugging away - getting the ball forward with good old fashioned work and sweat.

And then all of a sudden, your opposing team makes a play that they've already played a million times before. Still, you're just not prepared for it. Their play works - crushes right through you. The moment you even see the play starting, your heart sinks in that familiar tone and your muscles tighten in those same places, just like before. You're stuck. They score.

And, for the umpteenth time, you wonder why you're still playing this game at all. "How in the world," you wonder, "am I ever going to fight this same play of theirs? There's no way out. I don't see any options!"

And this is where your training comes in. It helps to learn how to play defensively as well as offensively. As time goes on, you'll learn which team members of yours are best for each kind of play. Sometimes you'll need all of them. Sometimes you'll need only one of them.

The more you play, the more you'll learn who to use and when. None of it will ever come naturally to you, though, unless you get in a good amount of playing time on the field with all of your players. Think about it.

When players try out for certain positions, the coaches watch them play first. You have to have time with your own team out there before you can really learn a lot about their dynamics - how they play and how they don't. That means seeing your team play on its own, without anyone else's help out there.

Which brings me to my very first training session.

- Keeping a Clean Team -

Yes, I do mean clean. On both levels. Clean of other people's players and clean of players who are substances and/or objects of addiction.

You will never know your team's current condition unless you know how many players you're bringing to the table or exactly how well each of them are playing until you finally get to see your team play *on its own.*

I know we've gone over this before, but it's worth going over again. You know more of your teammates now - you've spent time with them. There are nuances we can talk about now that we weren't ready for before.

If there's even one single foreign "player" helping out on your team, it will, it absolutely will, change *so* much of your team dynamics. You will never see them clearly. You will never know where you really stand, where you're really wounded, where you're really weak... until your team is clean. Sober. On its own.

Oh yes, I said sober.

Borrowing someone else's player to play in your stadium, on your field, is called codependency. Addiction merely means being codependent on a *substance* instead of a person. So if you need a player named Alcohol to finish a game, then your team is *not* clean. Not at all.

If you need your mother's input on every step of your life - crave it - can't make the decision in peace without it - you're probably codependent. If you need Oxy, Vicodin, Meth - the list goes on and on - to live out your day, every day - when your pain is no longer an issue - you're probably codependent.

Healthy relationships with these substances or people are when they come alongside your game only - in the assistant coach or cheerleader positions. They don't cross over the boundaries onto your field. I have lived such relationships. I have dealt with terrible physical pain - much more than a young person normally experiences - so I understand the beauty of pain relievers very well. I've also needed assistance from relatives or friends. There are times in life for that too.

So when I say "keeping a clean team," I don't say it lightly. I don't *mean* it lightly. Please turn to a professional when it comes to understanding the true differences between sobriety, addiction and codependency. My point is that this spring training is meant for an operational and working "clean" team only. It doesn't have to be a high functioning clean team, but it does need to be *clean.*

Now, I understand the difficulty of this. I understand your hesitations when it comes to codependency with people. What about the people you're leaning on that you don't even know you're leaning on? "What if I can't afford to live on my own salary or my own means?" "What if I'm scared?"

Don't worry. I've been there! And there's hope.

The point is for you to become as clean as you can at the start. It won't work otherwise. A young reader once worried that they only had a handful of other names on her first roster. She thought she should have more. She was right. There were others. But none that she could think of - until she started spring training. It opened her eyes to others and she had to stop and take the time to remove them as well before continuing on again.

This is natural. It's understandable. We are all just beginning at some point. Take my own beginnings, for example. It took me five whole years to cut every single tie with my worst abusers. "How in the world," you might ask, "did they come to be on your team?"

That's a great question! Because they operate best there. They insist on being on your team. They *teach* you to need them. They raise you in codependency. Abusers generally desire power over you, and where better to get such power, than on your team?

So when my day came - when I had to make the most important cut - I had a difficult time too. I ceased all texting. Then all phone calls. Then all emails! Can you believe it? Don't think I don't know how shocking such suggestions are to you! Here in California it's hard to find a fourth grader without their own earpiece, never mind a grown woman deleting texts she hasn't read, or blocking emails of those who share blood. So I fully empathize with the weight you may feel at the thought of ceasing any of those things.

But here's what happened. After I cut one - wow - the oxygen was rather surprising. The daily stress decreased much more than I thought it would. Then I cut the next. Again - oxygen!

It felt a bit like the action that occurs on a giant scale. The weight of the cords, chains and shackles are on a the left side of a great balance beam scale, the kind the lady of justice holds in her hand. The right pan holds the coins of my freedom. The lead far outweighed the gold.

The gold only existed because of previous work I'd done. The scales had shifted towards the freedom end of things for the first time... but would shift back rather easily if I wasn't super careful, or shift slowly back over time. Either way, the scales were only 'just' tipped in my favor after years and years of work.

But when I made my first cut, and ceased texting, I couldn't believe how much lead dropped away and how much gold was added to the right. And the more areas I ceased, the greater the scale shifted. It was dramatic. It became easier and easier to separate further and further from those who I was once bound so closely to. Much easier than you can even imagine.

So this is the good news; the more decisions you make, the faster the scale starts to tilt, the easier the decisions come.

And if the lady of justice analogy doesn't work for you - just think of it like a dirty front window on your car. It hurts your ability to *see* while you drive and therefore handicaps your *ability* to drive. If you pull over at a gas station in frustration and clean off 60% of the dirt, how easy is it to drive with that 40% of dirt left? Hard. You want the rest gone already. You just have to get it off, right?

Well, that's exactly the same math that happens when it comes to your teammates. The more you cut off of your team - the better your team gets at playing - the more it will want to play with its own team members only.

Now, one last thing before we move on, if you're interested.

There is such a thing as Codependents Anonymous (CoDA). I kid you not. And it's awesome. In fact, many people say that since all substance abuse is really just codependency with a substance, they say CoDA is one of the most foundational and important and central Twelve Step programs out there.

So if you feel you need more help in the area of keeping your team "clean," or even just more information about CoDA and what it looks and feels like, then look them up. Also, just an FYI here, but Twelve Step programs have gone global. There are online groups which not only help in getting you started, but can also help when you have certain time restraints, etc.

Alrighty. Let's get back to spring training.

I'd like to now go over some common tactics, skills and plays to improve your entire team out there, not just a single player or two. We're all different and we all face different teams, yes, but these are some of most common drills and methods of getting your team on the scoreboard, no matter where you come from or what state your team is in.

We'll dig into our offensive skills first.

- OFFENSE -

In football, when it's time for your team to play offense, it means, in the most basic of terms, that you 1. Have the ball and 2. Want to move it forward until it makes a touchdown in the end zone.

I have a feeling I made my football fans cringe with this definition. I also have a feeling I made my artistic and/or non-sports fans cringe as well. Ah well. I'm almost done. Bear with me.

This book is called *Touchdown*. It's all about how to make sure our ball gets moved towards our end zone. It's the only time you'll ever see a football player dance during a game. It's what this life is all about.

Making progress. Moving forward. Jumping for joy. And throwing that ball down onto the ground and being proud... incredibly proud... of what you and your team did to get there.

Every choice, every hard decision, every piece of sweat, cut and chain lead you right up to this moment. People know when you've made a touchdown. Better yet, *you* know when you've made a touchdown. And, just as in football, it affects the world around you. It really does.

I won't lie. Hell week is necessary, especially for those of us who don't, well, know what yearning is, for example. But it's not the *only* thing.

Here are some of the strongest plays we can make in order to "go against" our opposing team. Remember, our opposing team knows us really well. They are strong. Not only that, but they've been pushing us back for a really long while now.

So these plays I'm giving you are the ones with the "big fists," shall we say. These have the most gusto, the most power, the most punch for every penny we put in. Here they are in alphabetical order:

- ✓ An "About Myself" List
- ✓ Choice of friends, peers, community
- ✓ Change of habits
- ✓ Counseling
- ✓ Diet & Exercise
- ✓ Doctors
- ✓ Medication
- ✓ Tracking your body
- ✓ Twelve Step Program

Some of these may sound redundant and some of these may not seem so easy at first. Here are some explanations and clarifications for you.

An "About Myself" List

Okay, so this is a new term. It is completely my own invention and I'm including it more as a 'benefit of the doubt' measure. I created it for myself not very long ago, but it's made a big difference already, so I think you'll get a lot out of it too.

I believe that our western society is increasingly being separated into two categories: the meek and the strong, for lack of a better term. The strong lean toward the 'bully' qualities, though sometimes they just know how to get what they need or want better than others... so they do. They know how to take care of themselves.

Then there are the meek. The meek know how to take care of *others*. Many *live* to take care of others. They couldn't function with others. They like giving things away, or helping others more than is really normal or even healthy. They do it at their own expense. They are who we call "really nice" people.

They always listen. They love to smile. In fact, you've probably never seen them frown. We never ever consider their needs because they always seem so happy. They have a hard time saying no. This section, this exercise we're about to do - is for those people.

If you can relate to "the meek" I described, stay here and try this exercise with me. If not, feel free to move on to the next heading.

Now, my dear "meeks"... We're going to make a list that we carry around with us. At the top of it write "Things I've Learned About Myself." Now be sure to carry it with you - on your phone, on your device, on the pad next to your reading chair - just make sure that you have a list somewhere - or two or three.

Then start paying attention to the things that make you feel better.

I'm serious. If you catch yourself dancing or singing or humming during the day, immediately write down on that list what activity you were doing that made you feel good. If you catch yourself laughing, write down what you were doing that made you laugh. If you "finally feel better," or breath a sigh of relief or drop your shoulders... write down what you were doing that put you in that place.

Then make sure you read the list after a while - start to memorize it - and start to do those things when you are in a bad mood. I'm not kidding. You would be surprised. I call it my "Notes to Myself" and I say things like, "MUSIC!!! You LOVE MUSIC!!! PLAY IT!!!"

I never feel like playing it at the time, but I do it because my list says to do it and... hey - it works. My mind is either uplifted or distracted. Either way, it's better than where I was before.

Your opposing team loves it when you're "meek." Meek people never take care of themselves and they almost always lose. The only time they win is if someone insists they play their game for them. Losing teams *do not* make great givers, lovers or helpers. Learn to take care of yourself first, before considering helping the world around you.

Choice of Peers, Friends & Community

I don't know the key to success, but the key to
failure is trying to please everybody.
Bill Cosby

I love this quote. It includes family as well. If you've ever watched the TV show *Intervention*, or seen a movie about someone who has just left rehab, you'll notice that the addict is not the only unhealthy one. The last *Intervention* I saw spent a whole fifteen minutes of action just trying to get a mother to actually tell her daughter the words, "I love you." She just wouldn't do it. She kept replying, "We just don't do that in our family."

Ah yes. There are people in the world who would rather watch their daughter get high then open their mouths and say, "I love you." Things really do get this bad, everybody. An addict doesn't just appear out of nowhere. They come from a system that's very broken.

This is why so many who leave rehab are reluctant to hang out with their "old crowd." Like I said earlier, if we are unhealthy in one respect, then we attract people who fit in with that unhealthy behavior. Givers find takers. Takers find givers.

There is no doubt that the healthier you get, the more your friends will seem different to you, and you will gradually make new ones. Be prepared to watch your circles change, and for the better. This is always a good sign. Don't be afraid.

As much as your past will insist that you are the problem, you are <u>not.</u>

As one of my "old" friends raged and yelled at me through the phone, it finally hit me. I said, "We should probably take a break. It doesn't sound like either of us is feeling loved by the other right now."

And I hung up and cried, hard, harder than I ever had for or with a friend before. God, it hurt. Ripped me inside out. But I never heard from her again. And I didn't miss her like I thought I would.

My point is that sometimes our "friends" or our "community" is playing for our opposing team either sometimes or all the time. By removing them from the field, they can no longer block you from making a touchdown.

You won't believe how many new touchdowns you can make with this powerful skill - of changing your peers, friends, even family and community. It's a play that never fails - hands down.

Change of Habits

Winning is a habit. Unfortunately, so is losing.
Vince Lombardi

One year, when I was teaching high school, I went on two trips during Christmas break - one was to Vegas to visit family. I was treated to one of the Cirque du Soleil shows along with some other family sites and sides of Vegas.

The second trip was to LA, where someone on the freeway rear-ended us from behind while on our way to Griffith Observatory. When I returned to work, everyone asked me how my break was. For some reason I always replied, "I was in an accident."

By the end of the week I'd completely forgotten about my Vegas trip and I was in a bad mood. Somehow I caught myself, I think it was *Feeling Good*, so I changed my story and only answered everyone with the Vegas story. I was in a better mood by the end of the day.

This is not me throwing 'lipstick on the pig.' In reality, I really was oversharing with those I'd told about the accident - I felt safer answering with Cirque du Soleil.

Feeling Good has a plethora of new habits to try that you've probably never even heard of or thought of. It's a great resource. There are, of course, other kinds of habits I'm referring to here - from diet and exercise to your thought patterns. Candy, I've noticed, increases my pain and puts me in a bad mood, while oranges and calcium do the opposite. I made sure to write these observations on my "About Myself" list too, by the way.

Other habits include roads you take home, pictures you take, if you're spending time outside or spending time inside... even things like temperature play a huge role in how you play your game. Find out what temperatures your body thrives in (right now it's 64 degrees for me, can you believe it?) and do what it takes to be in that kind of environment so you can recharge, relax and be joyful energy.

Counseling

Do I really need to add on here? Well, just a little bit.

I don't know *anyone* that could not benefit from an excellent counselor or therapist. But, as I mentioned earlier, an excellent one is hard to find. Just because someone raves about them doesn't mean that they are right for you. So here are a couple of tips to follow when it comes to choosing the right one for you.

First, it only takes 1-3 sessions to know if you are with the right counselor. The more experience you have or the better you know yourself, the faster you will know. You should leave feeling heard every single time. If you don't - it's a big red flag.

Second, you should see significant progress within 6-8 weeks, assuming you're going once a week. You should be able to look at your life and say "here is where this is going better than it was before." There don't have to be improvement in a lot of areas - even just one will help. But there should be something you can point to and describe.

And finally, know that a good therapist might mean a bit of a drive or a lot of cash, depending on your insurance. If you need it, be sure to ask if they are flexible on their rate when you pay cash (it never hurts to ask, and don't be insulting by insisting on some seriously low number - be respectful) and second, if they are a long drive away, see if they would be willing to do every other week, but have two sessions back to back when you do meet. That way you can still have the benefit of enough time, but while spending less on gas.

It's not uncommon to find yourself just getting going when time runs out. Double sessions have been known to help with that, if they are available.

Doctors

Holy heaven how important doctors are! Especially in today's healthcare system! They can make or break your entire life. If you do not feel safe with doctors, please try and get some help with that. A good advocate is worth their weight in gold.

Much like my ACT therapist, my local neurologist was so thorough that he caught five injuries; three to the spine, that none of my doctors had ever caught before. Then his tests caught a rare disorder, along with... well, you know the drill.

My point is that he was my first *advocate*. When my insurance company dropped him, we stayed on with him and paid in cash. Do *not!* skimp on your doctor! Keep switching and searching until you find the one that's right for you... in every area of your health.

They aren't kidding when they say that knowing is half the battle. It is! And the more you know about your health, the more you'll know how to train your body and mind for the big game.

Tracking Your Body

Being aware of your body is practically a whole other book. I don't mean "aware" in any kind of transcendental form or any kind of New Age theology either. I mean "aware" to the point that you catch your body's red flags.

Our body is designed to send up flares to let us know that something is wrong. Today we almost never consider anything else other than pain as a red flag. Yes, pain is a red flag. Absolutely. But there are different types of pain. And do you know what they all mean?

Go online and print out a pain chart for yourself. Learn it. Know it. People usually overestimate or underestimate pain. One of the charts has faces that we make. Well, my face never changes - I had to hide pain to survive my childhood.

So the notes underneath the faces help me - like, "ability for normal activities is impaired." Well okay, yes, I'm having trouble standing up... so now I know I'm at level 7 or higher. Pain charts are an amazing utility. Be aware and be ready when your body sends up that kind of flare.

Your body also sends up other kinds of flares- from digestion, to swelling, to bruising, losing weight - even things like dry skin can cause so much more irritation than you realize. Then, when you treat it, stress you never noticed suddenly disappears.

Watch your body. Start learning it. Track things that concern you - you might be surprised, but then empowered. And, by the way, there's an app for that. There is. Whether it's taking medication, monitoring heart rates... anything at all, there's an app for it. So helpful!

Speaking of apps, ladies, track your monthly red flag, yes? The apps today are miraculous and the right ones can teach you so much about your body and how it changes throughout the month. I know people who literally plan their work weeks and/or month around their cycles, because they know when they'll have the energy to do their best work and when or if they won't.

Have any questions? Bet there's an app for that too.

- DEFENSE -

In some ways our defense strategies are similar to our offensive ones. Diet and exercise are always helpful in plowing down an opposing team, but they are also almost imperative when it comes to defense.

To be straight, when times get rough and I'm totally on the defense from my opposing team, I actually start taking *more* vitamins than when I am not. It's the same with certain medications too. Depending where we're at in life, certain skills and wisdom cross both of the training lines of offense and defense.

Defense, however, is when we *don't* have the ball. The opposing team does. And they are coming at us - hard, and fast. Let's face it. These are the times when we are the most disoriented.

I wish the game of life had whistles and guns and flags - all the things in sports that tell us when it's time to start the game.

It just isn't like that in our stadiums, is it? No. One minute we have the ball... and the next we don't. Just like that. And when our opposing team gets the ball they don't hesitate, do they? They grab it and come at us.

Ah, what a simple difference between our game and their, but oh, how it changes everything. We have to be only that much stronger. As such, I have recommended some rather unusual defense training exercises for your team:

- ✓ Blocking Bad
- ✓ Diet & Exercise
- ✓ Front Row vs. Back Row
- ✓ Heal All Wounds
- ✓ Medications
- ✓ Spiritual Battle
- ✓ Yes and No
- ✓ Let's flesh some of these out for you.

Blocking Bad

You've heard it a million times before from every corner of the globe in every single form a media there is: things are going "social." Like it or not, social media isn't going anywhere anytime soon.

Generational differences aside, the social networks can truly work to all of our advantages, but only if we know how to use them. If we don't they can very quickly and easily hurt us. Harm us is more like it. So we need to be savvy.

Yes, security settings are great, but let's face it; Google, Yahoo and Facebook all want your information so that they can sell things to you and sell information to others so that they can sell things to you too. Hence the widening gap between the classes.

But when it comes to your stadium and your field and the opposing team you have to face, the real threat is bullying. Social media provides people with a mask. And they can do awful, awful things with a mask. There's no fear. It's an epidemic.

I'm here to tell you that you *cannot* live by your in-person manners, etiquette and skills when you are online. Others don't. They live by different rules online. They say different things. They rarely do and say the same things both online and in person.

This is a hard lesson. *Do not* learn it the hard way. Do not be afraid of blocking somebody. Do not be afraid of hurting their feelings. Always err on the side of blocking instead of unfriending - they are less likely to notice and you are less likely to ever remember or relive their political views, their slight jabs, their ebbing peer pressure or their outright rudeness.

You have no idea how powerful a social media is - how much it can influence you. They've already done studies that show we are in a better mood off of Facebook than on it. I believe that's because we don't have any defenses at *all!* We were not taught to be defensive in social situations... but it's the most important skill you'll ever need to survive online.

Even when it comes to emailing - do not fear blocking someone's email. They don't receive a notice. Way too often we let others eat away at us with junk emails or mothering, smothering statements about how we *should* be living differently - from how many laps we did for exercise to what we're eating for dinner to who we are dating.

Stop treating your online world the way you would treat your offline world. You can never go too overboard when it comes to taking defensive and preventative measures online. Reporting, blocking and un-following are your best friends. Trust me.

Front Row vs. Back Row

While outlining your stadium I mentioned that you can't really choose who comes in and out of it. That's true to a point. First, you can totally change anyone's seat in your stadium. Second, you can have your security team escort them out.

Oh yes, they can climb up on the rafters and watch from a distance, but that's it.

It is perfectly normal to move people between different sections of your stadium as you grow, expand and learn. Just as we have times of weakness, so do others. There are times that we are not doing well and we accidentally come out side-ways on people.

They have the freedom to move you back a few or more rows during that time, especially when they themselves are having a difficult time too. Don't get me wrong - there are times we need each other to come alongside and help support the team closer to the sidelines.

But too often we don't take defensive measures when we should. We don't have to be mean about it. We don't even have to say anything. But it is healthy to protect your team and your performance by putting distance between you and others in your life when it is necessary.

Now. Let's talk about the *Others.* The ones we finally take off our field and put into the coaching section. And that was really hard to do, too. But it does not end there... no. It never does with the Others. And so it begins. You're still to close to them while they are in your coaching section to feel more love than stress and/or sorrow with them there. So you move them into the stands - in your front row.

Uh oh. They aren't taking that very well, are they? They're angry they aren't on your team anymore. They can't stand the distance. You feel even less love from then than you did before. You hold out as long as you can, you really, really try... until you're exhausted. Spent. You finally realize you're not playing very well because of them. They are draining you. They aren't happy for the touchdowns you finally did on your own.

They aren't happy *for* you. They aren't happy *with* you. So you finally move them back a few rows. You ask them questions to socialize instead of sharing about yourself. You put boundaries on the more intimate topics and only share the superficial ones.

It still doesn't work. Then slowly, you finally realize, they don't want you to win at all. They just want you to let them in. All the way. I'm here to tell you that it's okay to remove them from your stadium when this type of situation happens. These things do happen. We are human. We are not perfect. You're not the first one to have to do this... You are not alone.

Heal All Wounds

As advanced as we are in medicine and science, we are actually spiraling miserably into the habit of minimizing pain in our society.

We lose a celebrity. The news shares it everywhere and everyone posts and talks about it... then some people shamelessly makes some money on it... then we're on to the next story. We don't. Take time. To *heal*.

We need to heal! Fully! There are gaping half-open wounds everywhere - in all forms: physical, emotional and mental.

I'll never forget the surprising observation that stood out to me while watching a documentary on Bobby Kennedy. When JFK was lost to us, Bobby mourned for *six months*. How right this sounded. How 'just' it seemed to me. And we, the nation, gave him that time. He paced. He wandered. He stayed still. And he pondered.

When he took the podium again, the audience let him speak - slowly, evenly and with mighty big words and references. I remember it so clearly - I could see the wound, but I could also see the stitches. I could see he had healed. It was such a foreign look to me.

I don't believe we are allowed to mourn anymore. I don't think we're even allowed to heal a broken rib or a broken leg anymore. Our opposing teams are cheering wildly. Do you know how easy it is for them to pound us when we never fully heal from an injury?

If your doctor says ten weeks, take ten, not eight. If your body wants to sleep, let it sleep. Take the time off if you have to. *Get your sleep*. Be well. Listen to your body's flares. Listen to your doctors and your wise counselors... take *all* the time you need, not the time your opposing team would cheer for.

Spiritual Battle

If you are not of my faith or don't want to hear this, feel free to just skip ahead here. I'm not writing this to preach to anyone at all. I just have a lot of experience in this area and it would be shameful if I did not share it with those who need and/or want to hear it.

It's silly how much we talk about spiritual battles and warfare. If I want to get angry, I turn on a Christian radio station. Please don't freak. I most likely haven't listened to yours, but the ones I do hear are always offering the "slap on a smile" approach. Are you kidding?

The last broadcast I heard had a minister who said, "If you really want to be a witness, then you must always have joy in your heart. If you don't have it, repeat verse after verse about joy over and over again - claim joy and it will be yours."

Um. No. Spiritual warfare is just that. War. And considering it's against Evil, let's just go ahead and assume that the war torn landscape of the spiritual realm is a heck of a lot uglier than any kind of war we see on the face of this planet.

I have a lot of experience on this landscape. I have battle scars, a sword, weapons and a shield. I've dripped blood. I've taken blood. I, even as I write this, am at war on that plane.

Do not think that your opposing team's dark players are going to suddenly deflect off of you when you say happy words. There is power in scripture, no doubt, but one verse is not going to work every time. This is war. You can't go in there with the same defense strategy every time!

Here is my advice to you. When you think you are being attacked spiritually, which I can promise you is more often than you think it is, then you need to start acting like you are on a battlefield. Seriously. Get your mind, heart and brain on that field and start training, living and acting like a real warrior would.

Think the gates of Mordor. Think Vietnam. Think Afghanistan. Get real. Get dirty. And get wise. Ask for wisdom. Every warrior has a King. Follow Him. Not the radio. Their version leans towards band aids instead of blood.

When it comes to the spiritual realm, your best defense is seeing the battlefield clearly and to familiarize yourself with the great fire that is your inheritance. Be ready to fight, to war, to win.

Yes and No

The subtitle of the book *Boundaries* reads, "When to say yes, when to say no, to take control of your life." How well put. It really sums up the concept of boundaries very well.

That's because all boundaries, even ones like laws and county lines, are all constructed of two kinds of brick: the word yes and the word no. This is my property. Yes you may come on it. No, you may not.

This is my house. Yes, you may come in. No, please leave. This is my world. Yes, I will let you in a little bit and talk to you about my job and my care. No, I will not let you in a lot or talk with you about my relationships, children or finances.

Yes and *no*. The bricks that define all boundaries. We are usually good at only one of these words. We are either really good at saying yes to everyone and being, living and acting like everyone wants us to.... or we are really good at saying no.

We don't do anything we're asked to do. We don't let anyone in to our world, thoughts or lives. We have a very, very high wall built out of the word no.

Sometimes I think our touchdowns are almost completely dependent upon who and what we say these two words to. If we say yes to the wrong people or things, they get too close to our field or team and sabotage our game, causing us to lose.

It's the same way with the word no. We have to know how to use these two words in tandem. We have to learn how to say yes to the good and no to the bad and yes to people in certain areas, but no to them in others. It's such a delicate balance.

I'm still learning it.

The opposing team knows which one of these words is your

weakness. If you have a hard time saying no to people - oh my stars - they will come after you with a million different needy kinds of people and you will be overwhelmed and drown in their miseries and pain.

To win you have to be brave enough to say no. You have to dig deep within yourself and do something scandalous - like building a boundary with the world no. Or yes. Meeting new friends with healthier behaviors down the road will be difficult after your scars from those before.

It takes bravery to let them in. But I feel, and maybe this is just from personal experience, but I feel like the inability to say no is the more deadly of the two wounds. Saying yes to one person makes a huge difference in our lives. But saying no to twenty is so very much harder.

You may have to leave and try new communities. You might have to be brave and risk others' scorn or displeasure. Watch your game closely and see how often you make decisions based upon others' pleasure or displeasure. It's a dead-on sign of a weak no.

Remember, on an aircraft they insist you put your oxygen mask on yourself first, and then your child. It's the same thing here. You have to have a winning team first in order to be a good friend to others.

If your game is struggling, then that is where your focus must be. Learn to say no. Say it with grace; say it with finality, say it without extra reasoning or excuses and you will start to win. Then, and only then, will you enjoy friendships made of gold and silver, not rust and coal.

—

So there you are - some rather unorthodox methods to use when it comes to your team's defensive plays and skills. They are all tried and true however, and I think you might be surprised at how successful even just one of them are.

I think I might be underestimating you here though. You've gotten this far, haven't you? Straight on through *Hell Week*, right? Well then, you ladies and gents are the ones who are going to change the world with these words. I know it. I can see it.

It's a bit overwhelming too, because it's all of these offensive, defensive and retraining techniques, skills and outlooks that brought these words to you. Imagine what they will bring to your life, to the lives around you, to your children and your children's children.

What life. What joy. What love. I stand tall for you. Salute you. Cheer for you. You are always on my mind.

9 FOR THE WIN
I know where I'm going and I know the truth...
I don't have to be what you want me to be.
I'm free to be what I want.
-Muhammad Ali

Society, cultures, parents and certain worldviews are all known for their different kinds of "touchdowns." The games in these stadiums may vary, but they are still all built in the hopes of one single solitary thing: to *win*. Cheer. Explode. Fireworks! Celebrations. Even dancing... all because of that glorious score. Those amazing points. In football it's that rectangular box of turf & air called... the "end zone."

It is the same for us when it comes to our own personal stadiums. We may all be playing the same game, but everyone's end zone looks different. No single person's touchdown will look exactly like another's.

A winner, approaching the end of his road, will stand surrounded by the sum of all he has done, and it will look different from the sum of another man's life. A painter, an engineer, a coal miner, a housewife... the incredible celebration that takes place upon each touchdown, each win of a game, will look oh, so very different.

But getting there? The game? The process of winning and of making those touchdowns - that's what we share. Amazing players are amazing players. And no matter what part or parts we play in this world, those who are winning stand out. Brightly.

- The End Zone -

In order for any of us to ever see the inside of an end zone, we have to know *how* to win. There is hearing about how to win, learning about how to win and then there's actually *seeing* how to win. Any sports coach will tell you that it is much easier to learn how to play by watching a winning team *win*, than by watching a losing team *lose*.

So I'm going to help you learn how to both identify and then study winners when you see them. One of the most beautiful things about humanity is that no matter what country, city or culture you are in- the signs of a winner will remain the same. They will stick out to you. Stick out like a sore thumb.

You might not even like them when you meet them or see them operate in this world. You might find them to be obtrusive, separate or cold... I definitely did, in my early days. I couldn't figure out how to get their love or approval. They didn't accept my "bid" for drama. Neither did they let others walk over them. They knew how to fight for themselves and they never accepted help "just to be nice."

What I learned later is that they wouldn't join me, or others for that matter, in the game of codependency. I needed to be able to please them, help them or encourage them. I needed them to *need* me. Which really meant that I needed them to need or want one of my players for their own team.

When they wouldn't accept one of my players - when they functioned just fine on their own, I would be in shock. I felt scorned, hurt or confused. But they just wanted to *know* me. Just the person standing in front of them. They wanted to simply know who I was inside.

Or they simply wanted me to *do* my job, not *more* than my job. Time after time I would overwork myself at my jobs, or at least the jobs that would let me. Working in the church was such a bad idea for me. Being a wife, I now know that it calls for much more than physical intimacy.

But in the offices I worked in, the men needed me to do all the other things a wife did, and more. Oh, they didn't cross physical boundaries (much), but they loved my eagerness to please them and they let me fight game after game after game of theirs.

So when I met pastors, secretaries or ministers who did not want that from me, who simply wanted me to be a secretary and no more - not a counselor, advisor, helper, peacemaker or troubleshooter - I felt stabbed in the heart. I felt utterly rejected. I thought I'd done something wrong.

I had, in a way. I wanted them to want me to be more than was required of me. I wanted them to let me on their fields and help play their games. But they were winners, not me. They were healthy. And they wanted, in reality, a healthy relationship with me...

But I did not have enough self-worth or players on my team, to play my own game. I lived my life playing on everybody else's team, and simply loved watch their teams win! Oh! It was such a high. And so many people let me. They loved the help I gave them and they loved, even more, taking credit for my team members' work on their fields.

Every member of my immediate family expects my team members on their fields. They raised me this way. I became good at it. No, I became an *expert* at it! And wow, did their lives thrive when I gave all my wisdom, talent, advice, love and stability to each of their teams and relationships.

When I left, things fell apart. I didn't just rock the boat, I practically capsized it. And to this day, even on their own, my siblings long for me and need me to come back in that capacity for which I was raised. Their own core training wired them to see me that way. And since "mother and father" didn't approve of my absence, then neither could they.

They blame their inability to tame *their* rough seas on *my* absence, not on their inabilities. How I ache for their own team members to grow strong enough to play their own games, and to finally see me whole, to give me credit for what I have done and to be happy for me for finally winning some of my own games. But alas, that day may never come.

But even though I'm stronger now, I still remember those winners I talked about from years ago. The ones who didn't need me. The ones who had all the teammates they needed and made a lot of touchdowns too. They all stand up, in a row, in my mind. Like I said, winners stick out. You remember them. And the fact is that none of them were harsh with me. None of them were rude.

They were neither mean, nor 'cold' really - they just didn't fit with me. Their core training gave them excellent healthy boundaries and a complete and operational team that knew its strengths. They couldn't lose if they tried.

I'm starting to be on the other side of it now. I'm starting to win. I'm becoming whole and healthy. And I'm seeing others who are like the old me. Or others, who are not the helpful cheery type, but the mothering pushy type. They push their team members onto your team.

Oh, how it stabs me a bit, when I see the bitterness in their eyes when I don't let them in. I hear the chill in their voice when I now say *no* instead of *yes* and I know what they want from me. But I just can't give it to them. Any of them. The sweet helpers or the parental pointers. Not anymore. The cost is much too great.

We are all made differently though. We are all raised differently, and those that give us our core training have also shaped and molded how we interact with others - how we view them, how safe we feel around them and what we expect of them. And because of this, you may not have had any of the experiences with winners that I just listed above.

You may have found winners to be the exact opposite - warm, friendly and compassionate. We will soon find out. For now, I will do my best to help you see these touchdown-makers from afar - with a different and separate set of eyes.

I'll help you learn to be on the lookout, so that you will not only recognize them when they appear, but you will also be able to study them, learn from them and observe them, with or without ever even speaking to them. Saying hello never hurt anyone, of course, but for now it's simply more important that you know them when you see them.

Here are some of the characteristics every winning team will have, regardless off race, color or economic status.

Joy

The very first sign of a person who lives their life on the other side of the goal posts is *joy*. I don't mean charm. I don't mean cheery. I don't mean giddy and I don't mean smiley. I mean joyful.

Full of *joy*.

I once heard someone say that the most common place to find examples of joy is in children. Imagine this with me. You know that look a baby has when they experience joy - the one that changes their whole face and arms and hands? When they start pumping or jumping up and down?

Like when you play peek-a-boo with them or shake a rattle for them or make a silly face for them... they get that huge wide mouthy grin that seems to take up their whole face and then their arms circle round and round in their little baby-like claps, with totally open hand and extended little fingers.

They jump up just that fraction of a bit, with excitement and bubbly movement. Yeah. That's it. That's joy.

Delight. They are absolutely delighted. You know exactly what I mean. You can see it right there in front of you, can't you? Practically hear the diaper smushing up and crinkling down as the baby pumps their chubby little legs. Or maybe you hear that amazing little miracle of a giggle-gurgle. Oh!

Joy.

Don't see that very often in adults, do you? Yeah, it looks different - we don't circle our whole arms and clap with hands wide open (much), but joy is joy. And it can radiate from anyone anywhere. As long as they are winning.

Many of us lose joy, as we enter into adulthood. People say responsibilities are what weigh us down - life and the opposing team. That's true. Life is much harder when you are playing the game out there on your own. But if you learn to use all of your teammates and you are winning, you'll find that joy isn't lost - it's abundant.

This is *not* to be confused with charm. Charm is a verb. It is something done *to* you. It comes out of a person not because of *joy*, but because of *need*. Here are some of the things people emit charm for.

They *need* you to think one or more of the following about themselves:

- They are trustworthy.
- They are safe.
- Their way is the best for you.
- They know what you want.
- There's nothing wrong with them.
- They are important.
- They know what you want.
- They know what they want.
- They should be followed.

- They should be liked.
- That they aren't breaking any rules or hurting anyone when they do.
- They must be listened to.
- They are giving you all the information you need to know.
- They are doing the right thing when they skew the truth.

The list goes on and on. I know one young woman who, at every sign of weakness, starts smiling or giggling. Start talking a serious subject, start talking a vulnerable one and she will blush and smile.

Girls and young men who blush and smile easily are not happy. They never are. In fact, they are quite angry. Almost enraged. But their anger is so very, very deep down that they would never admit it. They would never believe it, actually. But bring up any kind of criticism, or question any kind of decision, and they will smile, blush, turn away and in many cases, tear up or cry.

Their whole facade is to present themselves as a healthy, whole and winning person, who has it all, knows it all and can help all. But they cannot be questioned. Ever.

A winner welcomes questions. They don't "listen to respond." They "listen to understand." What a huge difference.

Please be aware of charm. It's not just car salesman who use it anymore. Choir kids to narcissists to sociopaths... they are everywhere. And none of them are full of real joy. Joy is full of openness, curiosity, discussion and balance.

So very often in these cases, these people are overly cheery out of a need for *distraction*. They want to be distracted. They need to be distracted. They don't like serious things, problems or conflict.

Joy, however, is the exact opposite of distraction. Winners are joyous because of what they find in reality.

Joy holds hands with *reality*.

Remember that. Any other kind of cheer is simply false advertising. A winner has to embrace reality in order to win the game. A winner has to be able to see all of his opponents on the field. A winner is open to all the bad and the good in this world and is extremely aware that they themselves are fallible. Fallibility, reality and... *joy* - a winner does make.

117

Compassion

*Wisdom, compassion, and courage
are the three universally recognized moral qualities of men.*
Confucius

Ah, poor Confucius. He would be shocked by us now. Even so, I believe he beautifully states the heights man really can climb. I personally feel there is a war being raged against these three very qualities. But we can fight back. Always. All we have to do is recognize these "sales pitches" against such qualities when they come, and work hard to be the exact opposite. We have in the past. Why not again?

I point out compassion out of the three qualities of wisdom, compassion and courage because, well, you are already "wise" for reading this far. And making any of the changes here will take "courage" automatically. Once you've taken steps in these two areas, it's very easy to see them in others. It doesn't take much.

(Unless, of course, you fall for the internet. That's the *opposite* of wisdom. Anyone in the world can post on the internet. Imagine walking into a symposium on nuclear physics. Walk up to the podium and take a look around the room. Just by looking at everyone in the audience, you know who the crazies are. Or, let me put it this way - you know who you would like to discuss things with over lunch, and who you would not.

Well, the majority of the people posting on the internet now are the crazies. The ones you wouldn't want to share a lunch with. Think about it. They aren't heard in the real world. People on the streets and in the workplace rarely listen to their rants. So they go online, where we all magically consider them to be well founded, well rounded, educated and justly supported.

Bull. Everyone who you wanted to eat lunch with? They left the cafeteria a long time ago, tired of arguing with people who know nothing. The crazies are out there chatting and commenting away, trying to hit a home run with a banana, not a bat. And we are listening! Crazy! *Not* wise.

I'm just saying... in case you're falling for the internet... Poor Confucius...)

Back to the third quality he lists. Compassion is *not* so easy to spot. It's a bit different from wisdom and courage. Society may be warring against wisdom and courage, but it isn't doing so when it comes to compassion. Not directly, anyway.

Instead society has wound the definition of compassion around its finger and then blurred it all over the place. Compassion is not so easy to see these days. Almost impossible in some states. You will have to look a bit more closely. Again, this is an area where you might a think a person is being cold instead of compassionate.

Listen in... When I say compassion, I don't mean bleeding hearts. I'm not kidding. Please don't take compassion to mean martyrdom. I really mean quite the opposite. Having compassion doesn't mean 'putting others first.' In fact, putting others first is one of the first ways to *lose* compassion.

Yes, there is the saying of "do unto others," but people forget that it also says, "as you would have done unto you." You know what this means? That means that healthiness is wishing and willing someone to have a successful team... while taking care that your own team wins too!

It doesn't say "hurt yourself in order to help others." No. Compassion means being able to *see* others. See their positions, their pain, their perspectives and their rights - without needing to jump onto their field and do the work yourself.

Compassion is the willingness to see another person's field - the whole field - teammates and opposers alike, and feel for them. Empathize with them. Understand them. And then, if that team is willing to let you, come alongside them, to their sidelines, and coach them, help them and be willing to *know* them.

Sometimes knowing a person's team is all they need. There aren't a lot of people out there willing to do so anymore. They have no compassion these days. It shocks me, how accustomed we've become to being cruel to one another in order to make ourselves feel better.

An example? A son finally tells his mother than his cousin sexually molested him as a child. The mother minimizes it. Trivializes it. She says, "Oh, boys will be boys at that age." This is the *opposite* of compassion. Cruel and abusive, more like.

A woman at an intimate dinner with friends finally confesses that she has memories starting to come back to her during therapy. She is remembering abuse by her father. It clearly causes her to choke up a bit. A friend, unable to handle the reality, asks instead if these "memories" are really memories at all? That perhaps the therapist has created some where there were none. This is cruel!

Horrific! And the absolute *opposite* of compassion.

A neighbor's dog keeps escaping the fence and running into your yard and barking, loudly, at your door. You are scared. You explain that dogs frighten you, badly. They have, for as long as you can remember. The neighbor thinks you hate dogs. Your friends defend the dog. You are left feeling trapped, unheard, scared and traumatized. This is the *opposite* of compassion.

Compassion is our ability to see where others are coming from, hear them, and empathize with them. It doesn't mean giving advice. It doesn't mean fixing the problem. It doesn't even mean sending money. It means staying on center, and making a healthy choice, out of true love and truly justified and adult concern, to listen to, pray for or act on a certain situation. It's a choice. Not compulsive. And I haven't seen it in a long, long, long time.

What have we come to? When we cannot listen in silence, without correcting, denying or fixing a person's mourning?

May you see compassion in those who are winning, and may you start winning yourself so that others too may learn what true compassion is.

Being Present

A person who is 'present' is very much in their body and "checked in" wherever they are. For example, if I'm in line at the pharmacy and my mind is elsewhere, thinking about my kids or my pottery or my upcoming exam, then I'm not really "in" line. I'm "checked out" to a certain extent. I'm there physically, but I'm not there mentally.

There are some who aren't even thinking about anything. Their mind is in space, blank or on hold. People used to call it being "spaced-out," but that term is long gone, mostly due to the fact it's become quite normal and accepted in everyone from children to co-workers to spouses.

Video games, pornography and excessive texting or web surfing have most definitely ushered in the absolute largest movement of being checked out. It's become a way of life for some people. It's often used as means of escape or avoidance in relationships. But oh, does it cause so much pain.

Everyone who is checked out has someone else filling for them on their fields. A partner, a family, a parent is filling in and plays their game for them. It drains them though. We weren't built to do another person's living for them. So they lose their own games as a result.

That's why you hear people tell a parent that they have to let their kids grow up or get their own place. This only happens when it's clearly obvious that the parent is playing on their kid's field. They are taking all the punches meant for their kid, while they are *all* taking all the punches in their *own* stadium!

What these parents don't realize is that once their kids are out on their own, they have no one left to play on their field. They suddenly have to wake up to make it. They are forced to finally get their own teammates on their fields.

But a person who is not only playing their own game, not anyone else's and has all of their own teammates on the field in full uniform? Those people are not only present, but they fill the room. As one friend put it, "you feel the weight of them."

Ah, I love that term. "Feel the weight of them." Can you imagine walking into a room, so present, so fully in your own body, with all of your teammates jam packed across your huge field, tall, strong and mighty, with the force and will and weight of all that you have done, the weight of your training and the weight of your touchdowns... can you imagine walking into a room this way?

They shall feel the weight of you, alright. As you have felt theirs when you see them. They walk in power, love, not anger or dominance, but wisdom and strength.... shah...

They are *expanded*. They aren't just in their bodies - they go past their fingers and toes. Present people can make heads turn when they walk by. Their feet are firmly grounded into the floor. They stand with confidence, without fear. They are whole.

They react quickly because they are very much "in" the moment. If you trip, they catch you. If you start choking, they will be the first person in the room to react.

A person who is present is a powerhouse of sorts, especially in this new world of empty people. They have all of their teammates on their field. All of them. And they are ready to play. Oh, the power of playing your field, filling your game with wins and touchdowns and defeats of your opposing team.

When you finally get there and someone jabs you in a wound - thrusts a knife into one of your buttons - you are able to grab it just before it strikes and there is a nick instead of a cut, a win instead of a defeat. Oh. The joy, the freedom and the power of your team. Trained, huge, strong and ready - at bay, waiting for the call.

I'm shocked at myself, at times. I can't believe how embodied I am. I was on the rink the other day, in new skates and wobbling. And do you know what happened? One of the pros in the rink comes right by and swipes at my skate! Can you *believe* it! A *pro*!

Now, she did not do this on purpose. She was simply chatting with a friend. But she wasn't paying attention. She's actually quite arrogant, as a few of them are. And so, while not looking, she takes a curve and rams her right skate right through my left ankle.

And do you know what happened? I, *I*, didn't fall... *she* did! She started to wobble and guess what... my left hand shot out and snatched her right hand so hard and so steady that she instantly regained her footing... along with a look of stark shock upon her face.

I don't think she's wobbled in a long *long* time. And I'm pretty darned sure she's *never* been saved by a novice. Well, I should say - I'm pretty darned sure she's never fallen because a *novice* was more grounded into the rink than she was.

Guess who else was shocked - me! I mean, my left foot barely even felt it. I literally heard it say aloud, "you talkin' to *me*?" and just watched in proud defiance as it let the girls skate go "bling!" bouncing right off it like a tin can.

My, my, my, my, *my*! Guess I've gotten good at being in my body. Being present. A long time ago my doctor said to practice imagining redwood roots extending from me deep, deep into the ground. That's because we tend to tense upwards when we are off-center, overreacting or out of control... emotional, let's say, to a negative degree.

I've practiced those redwood roots. Deep deep into the earth. Wow. I think he'd be proud. They knocked off a skate and managed to have my hand shoot out before I knew I'd even been hit. Dang, my team's gotten good. And I started way, way, *way* back in the line. So you can get there too. Others already are. Keep an eye out.

You will feel the weight of them.

Freedom

I may live in "the land of the free," but I don't think it looks like that very much anymore. We have amazing cities, clean water and an abundance of food and goods.

But somewhere along the way, goods piled up into debt, food

piled up into obesity and health issues unfolded everywhere and our city infrastructures - after a long period of newfound professionalism and ethics - are becoming dirty again. Corrupted. Worse than the "old days." And it's happening fast.

In all of this we've become an increasingly shackled nation. Either by politics, anger, vanity, finances, family, fashion or joblessness, the roots of discontent are lifting their way up to wind around our wrists. But we "survive." We say that we make it. We lie to ourselves.

We let bad customer service, rotten food, burnt bread and tainted water in and don't say the word no to anything - not politicians, not kids, not teenagers, definitely not college kids. Let me stand corrected. We *do* say no to some things now.

We are starting to say "no" to anything that even resembles a law. And we tell ourselves that everything works out in the end, and that everything that happens was "meant to be." And we stay silent, silent, silent... letting all that was once fought for die in the name of self. The fat, swollen belly of *self.*

Free people feel differently. They most definitely do not play by our rules. New these rules may be, but we've completely white washed any history - any sense of what came before technology, waste and gluttony - so we hate the free. We think they make us look bad. But we *see* the free. We can't look away. That's for sure.

There's this crisp cold fresh air about them. You feel things slightly crackle around them. Like a wind shifting your hair up, flipping through your clothes.

They do crazy things. When they tell you their next step, you look at them sideways. Your head tilts a bit when you are around them or listen to them. You can't help but study them, even unconsciously. Your mind, in a corner, asks itself... *What's different here?*

Freedom. Oh, how it stands out. The people who are *free* are okay with the consequences of their actions. They are happy, even in their days of discontent, which we all as humans face. Free people are ready for fights. They know what's wrong and they know what's right.

But they are okay with our differences. They don't demand anyone be as they are. They are *free.*

They live and live hard. Completely. Without conformity. So they stick out. Like a sharp breeze across dandelions - it's hard to see them go. You want to take them with you. You want to see your own world through their eyes.

Freedom. I don't think of it as *ringing* as so many say, when it comes to our lives. I think of it as expansion. Honesty. The very opposite of a mask. But put many free people in a room and heck *yes* you'll hear it ring!

Freedom. When you have it, you'll start to think outside the box. You'll start to re-see the world. You'll stop assuming the whole of a picture or a window dressing is captured in whole by its caption below, or its title or its description.

You'll see it and study it and make your own title, your own words, and your own descriptions for them, according to how it strikes *you* - not someone else. It doesn't mean another description is wrong. You're simply free. You're free to both listen and learn *and* think on your own. You can do both. Like we used to.

Freedom. It's a forgotten term. But you will know it when you see it. And, I believe, it goes hand in hand quite often with curiosity.

Curiosity

Curiosity is one of the most universal qualities children are known for. They ask so many questions. They want to know so many different things. Sometimes they sound like an Encyclopedia Britannica with all the zany crazy things they know when their curiosity is allowed to thrive and grow. It's crazy. It's part of who we are.

Again, I don't believe it's meant to be lost on our way to adulthood... only toned, refined and developed according to how each of us is uniquely made.

And so curiosity looks different in adulthood. It's much more centered. Purposeful. Whether we know it or not. You can spot winning person's curiosity a mile away. When they are on a guided tour of a place, they are either very close to the tour guide, or way in the back, off to the side, looking and studying and kind of 'sniffing out' the surroundings - catching little things here, there and everywhere. They peek, they lean, they look up and they take odd photos.

Oh wow, do I ever love curiosity. It has fed my soul a million times over. Because once I was free of the inner critic and judge, I found I didn't have to obey its voice or live by certain rules. That's a big change from my first years as an adult. Guided tours and monuments brought me much more shame than freedom.

It is extremely rare that a childhood is *all* bad. As in, every waking moment-shaft of light-and-corruption bad. I may have suffered severe abuse on all levels, but there are things that were not completely poisonous.

For example, I was taken to a million museums and parks. I am grateful for this, because I learned while studying education that a child's test scores directly correlate to how many miles from their home they have been, and upon how many times over the span of their life.

Now, that's not the only thing affecting a child's scores, but I may not have enjoyed my classes as much as I did in school, or I may not have yearned to suck the meat and marrow out of every bone and dish UCLA had to offer when I was there. Half my learning didn't even happen on the page there. I loved learning. I thirsted for it.

But I did not enjoy it nearly as much as I could have. I did not gain from it even remotely as much as I could have. And I most certainly did *not* pick up on all the complements, implied suggestions and even downright forthright declarations that I had gifts and I should be using and developing them - in fullness and strength.

But alas. Good things in a tortured home only go so far. I am grateful for the introduction to landmarks and tours that could be taken. But I did not do them much... not for years and years on my own. In fact, it was not unless I experience hell week and then took several courses of spring training that I finally found myself able to enjoy a museum.

I was finally free to be curious again.

As a child, though, I didn't find joy or freedom in any of them when taken there. As a family member once pointed out, the albums from those days feature our dark faces upon the most splendid of backgrounds. I wasn't surprised though. I wasn't really free to be curious.

I thought I had to listen to what the tour guides said, because I thought that whatever was chosen for him or her to say by those who "know best," would be the information I not only *should* know, but I should learn it by heart. It was the best the place had to offer. And I knew that I'd have to remember these cold (for me) facts because I would be quizzed hard throughout the night on whether or not I was listening. Sigh.

Curiosity is not like this! Not in childhood and not in adulthood either. Curiosity is something you have to become friends with - you have *got* to learn it. Because it's one of the most powerful and visible characteristics of a winning team.

Curiosity does a myriad of things for your teammates. It grows them, heals them and inspires them. It's a *vital* part of a thriving team, I swear. Sometimes I think curiosity is really just the world "living" for short.

I just do. I really do.

Let me give you an example. Museums. For a long, long time I did not go to museums once I stepped into adulthood. That's because, as I mentioned, I never enjoyed a single experience. I remembered the museums alright, but I never wanted to step foot in one again.

A few years after my ACT therapy, I had stretched my new wings a bit. We started taking road trips. Then we started taking uncharted and unplanned road trips. Then we started stopping in the middle of the road trips just to take a look at a cactus we saw or get a better view of the clouds, the sunset, the rain, the land.

The more we stretched our new wings, the more unconventional we became. We almost never read the signs telling us about the tectonic plates or the volcanic ash. It's just not our thing. What a huge break from the strict rules of my family. To be honest, I'm still always shocked at how well fed I am just looking at an interesting pattern of sand instead of the plaque that tells me how the sand got there.

The curiosity of a winning team breaks a lot of rules. Because we're all different. We are all inspired by different things. We are all satisfied by different information. When my husband sees a blinking hat at a theme park, he freezes mid-walk and starts trying to figure out in his head how it's made.

I'm used to it, but I'm not curious about that at all. It doesn't even enter my brain, how a blinking hat's made. It's just an annoying hat in my way during the fireworks show. Period. But when I see cool shelving in a store, I have no problem veering over and moving whatever clothing or racks I can to get a good look at how it's built into a wall. I soooo want to know. I love installing shelves. I love staging. But that's not Nick's thing. He really doesn't care.

But we are both very, very curious. So start looking around your world. During a tour, look for the people who stay very close to the tour guide and/or ask really good questions. They tend to be either bossy and/or parental, or they are really and truly curious. You can tell that they want the information for themselves, alone - purely individual curiosity.

The other place you will find people with winning curiosities are at the edges of a guided tour. They are the people who stand apart from the pack, sneaking and leaning and bending to look at the surrounding around them. They whisper a question or duck down to read an answer... they don't interrupt the tour, or break any rules - but they aren't bounded by the guided tour's script.

It's not that these side-walkers are bored. They are just curious about other things than what the tour guide is saying. Just because they don't care about hearing what year the building was built, doesn't mean they aren't feed and strengthening their team members by studying the woodwork or the floor tiles or the edging.

Now that we've found some museums we like, Nick and I have noticed more and more that there are people who do both. They ask questions or they stay close to the tour guide or they take little side-adventures - or they do all three. Curiosity is respectful and it does have boundaries. It isn't outlandish or oafish or rude. It's simply curiosity - it will look almost childlike to you. It will fill them with excitement. And excitement feeds your team a hearty meal.

So another way to spot curiosity in someone is excitement. Excitement in adulthood is rare, if you think about it. But those who are curious? Oh how easy it is to excite them! Think about the look on someone's face when their curiosity is peaked. Curiosity always comes with a side of excitement.

———

Joy, compassion, being present, freedom and curiosity... I love these people. I know that they are winning, yes, and that's great. But honestly - look at this list of qualities. Who wouldn't want to talk to them? Who wouldn't want to hear what they have to say?

I love meeting them. They are a joy to be around. Even for a short period of time. I always leave feeling grateful for the time I spent with them. I always learn something. My mind always feels expanded. They've seen so much and yet they need nothing from you nor do they need to give something to you. It's like sunlight.

You know they're human. You can tell that they've taken hits. They have their own stadiums, their own opposing teams and their own weaknesses. And yet here they stand. Upright and winning. And I bet you a million bucks their lives show it.

The media may make fun of such qualities, but they aren't reaping the rewards of any kind of touchdown off camera. Not ones that bear more fruit and more touchdowns in the process.

- Of Children -

This is a surprise section for me. My book was completely outlined before writing it, but when I was doing some extra research for the word curiosity and on children, I ran across something that astonished me.

Wherever the words *curiosity* and *children* appeared, so did a few others. Repeatedly. And do you know what those other words were? Joy and freedom. Everywhere. Children have joy, freedom and curiosity. Joy, freedom and curiosity!

The subtitle of this book was already written before this research: *How to Score Curiosity, Joy and Freedom in Adulthood.* How fascinating that my book about success and happiness in *adulthood* would culminate in achieving those same things that permeate the world of *children*! Healthy children, of course. The entire idea is still twisting my brain a bit.

How in the world could this be possible? I never set out to advocate child-like behavior. Am I?

And then I thought of these famous words, which you yourself might have already done at the mention:

Truly, I say to you, unless you turn and *become like children*, you will never enter the kingdom of heaven. Whoever humbles himself like this child is the greatest in the kingdom of heaven.
Matthew 18:2-4

I first heard about this quote when I was a young girl. I remember it well because, for the life of me, I could *not* understand what the heck He meant. I mean... what??? Why in the world would you ask us to act like *kids*???

I won't lie. My reaction never changed. It remained the very same for all my life. I'm pretty close to the Man and I've asked him a lot of questions and to be honest, I just never asked Him about *this* one because, well, hey - where would I even begin?

And then today happened. During my research. I scrolled and I read and I read and I scrolled and read and on and on and I'll tell you straight up:

First, I panicked. "I can't write a book saying watch people who act like children! How in the heck did *that* happen? Oh no! Wait, what if people---"

Oh.

And there you go. That was my answer. *Become like children.* It took decades, a rather amazing collection of unique and vulnerable life lessons plus the writing of an entire book on adulthood to finally catch the meaning. To open my eyes. And to write a book outlining how to do *exactly* that... without even knowing it!

Because I don't just list joy, freedom and curiosity, do I? No. I also list compassion and being checked in. Those are very adult qualities.

But I think there is a reason He said "become like children." The fact that healthy children across the world are known for their joy, freedom and curiosity means that they are qualities we were *all born with*. I don't think we were ever supposed to lose them, do you?

Boiled down to it: we were born with joy, born with freedom and born with curiosity. And on our way to adulthood we lose every single one. We aren't supposed to. It's not how we were made...

And yet we do. How many adults do you know who actually have these qualities? Why do we lose them? Why are they crushed, mangled or removed from us the older we get?

And now I realize that this is exactly why He asked me to write this book. It is a step by step guide to bring those gems we were created with, back into our lives.

"*Unless* you turn and become like children..." we *lose*, don't we?

We lose the game. We lose life. We lose the joy, the curiosity and the knowing.

Let us claim our inheritance. Let us get back to what we were born with. Let's grow up and not only be all we were meant to be, but shine and glow in the knowing... in the key... in the *answers*. Hard though they may be. But help is, and will always be, here.

- Blueprints -

Knowing how to spot a winner is great. It shows you that they are out there, that it is possible to win, that others have made it to the big show. Wonderful. So what's it like to be them? Remember, joy, compassion and being present are just symptoms- just *signs* to let you know that you've got a winner on your hands.

But try to be full of joy, compassion or awareness only? Try to shortcut your way to the finish line? And you'll find yourself full-stop super early on. No, all these symptoms that you can look out for are simply the leaves on a winning tree, not its trunk. So let's examine the trunk now, instead of the symptoms that make a winner, shall we? Let's start with...

You.

You are one of a kind. I know, I already hear the groans... "Oh Lord, here she goes! Here come the gift shop sayings!" It's okay. Give me just a few more sentences here.

My husband works on CNC machines. They are big huge machines that swallow up a chunk of metal, hold the piece in its mouth and let a trillion different kinds of drill bits eat away at it until it is one solid piece of... something. It's either the wheel of a motorcycle, the metal part of a prosthetic joint or the cylinder of a small ball bearing. Once the drills have done their work, the CNC machine sprays the metal part that's left down with water and then spits it out in a wonderful Star Wars-like fashion, with large doors opening and clouds of steam bursting north.

Now, my husband's job is to make sure that he programs those millions of drill bits to make sure each one of the final products that are spit out are exactly alike. Of course, that's not easy. It's a crazy job. They have measuring tools that measure *millionths* of an inch. I'm serious. Millionths!

Ouch. I can't even imagine touching any part of it. He loves it.

I am a writer. Which means we are different. We are not at all like those identical pieces that are being artfully created and *whooshed* out of a machine. Instead, we are incredibly different from one another. If you have been married for any amount of years, or have raised your fair share of children with love, then you know - we humans are all *so* different, family or not. We just *are*.

Our DNA, I feel like, is just the start of our differences. It is my belief that each of us was built - not by a CNC machine - but by a carpenter, by a sculptor, kind of like Michelangelo. Michelangelo knew all he needed to know about the rock and the art it held within before he touched it.

He already saw, felt and sensed the beauty, the nuances and the shapes within the rocks before he even began to smooth them out. You should read his poetry sometime, yes? It's a bit of a dive into the less ordinary or well lit part of the literary world, but read him nonetheless. Consider it an adventure.

Back to us. We are *couture*. If you are strictly a football fan then look it up. Couture. We are hand made. Designed. For a very specific line of work at the very least, or small niches of many different worlds at best.

I always think of us as tools. There is the world we live in - the time and place into which we are born. And in that time and place that is set before us, we were woven specifically to help the world work *then*, but only in that puzzle piece of a space.

I have no idea what your piece in this puzzle of today's world looks like. I have no idea what you were meant to solve, change or enlighten. I don't know who you were designed to be - I don't know what a physical manifestation of you in the actual world of couture would look like. But I *do* know two things. And I know them by heart.

- ✓ You are meant to be *more than one* sort of tool, swath of fabric or type of pen stroke throughout the entirety of your life.
- ✓ And I know that you have hardly discovered, at *all!* all of what you were designed to be.

These are truths I've learned, and learned hard - not just through my own experiences, but through yours as well. I've traveled. I've listened. I heard. I understood. And I've seen. If you really listen, listen to yourself, down deep and quietly, you'll know I'm right.

Too often we are driven off course by someone else telling you to be something else. Too often another voice plays throughout your life and throughout your mind and whispers in your heart, saying the word "no" or bringing doubts against those special and unique talents we were born with in order to fit where we are supposed to in this place and time.

Most of us are driven off course by such voices or influences throughout our lives. I still remember when I was doing really well in dancing - shining and burning the brightest... that's when the flurry of voices from all different sources came against my dancing.

I no longer believe I was just built to be a dancer. I was built to be much more than a dancer. But a dancer I was built to be. There is no doubt about that. Yet, wow, a lot of doubt came my way when I began to truly shine.

For those of us who are not used to shining in our very own unique niche and for those of us who aren't naturally in tune with how different the part we are supposed to play from those around us is, there is a reason for it. There is a reason we don't know our roles. There is a reason our "roles" tend to be those in the same fields as our parents and our families. There is a reason we fear the world outside of what those before us have known.

For us, when we start to stray too far off the path *they* are comfortable with us taking (note that it has nothing to do with whether *we* are comfortable or not with that path), then we find resistance. Doubt. Fear. Work.

We don't find joy. We don't find pride. We don't find excitement. They have none for us in the place of our genius.

My challenge to you and the challenge of this entire book really, is to discover your blueprint. I can pretty much guarantee that if even 1% of this book rang true at any spot, or hit home in any way for you, then you have a 99% chance of having no clue what your blueprint looks like.

No. Clue.

Don't be dismayed. It's exciting actually. Just as a parent can become excited at getting to know their son or daughter as they grow, so can you get excited about discovering your blueprint.

Too many of us think we have to know the blueprint first. That's not true at all. I have finally figured out that I will still be learning new corners of my blueprint until I die. I look forward to it. It's been a delight and it has grown my love for both the carpenter and for my life in the discovery.

And the only way to discover it, is to become an adult first. Once you start scoring touchdowns, your opposing teams will weaken and the amazing characteristic of a winning team will start filling your life.

Then and only then, in my experience, will you, after living free for a few years, start to see edges of your blueprint. Your true design. Your one and only puzzle piece that no one, not even your mother or your father could have imagined.... no one but the carpenter who created you knows.

Because you weren't made to be *one* thing. You were made to be *many*. And unlike a simple puzzle piece, we are much more like cloth - divine cloth - complicated and wound and whole and different and frayed and impeccable.

Blueprints.

If I could ask for only one thing in this book, it would be that you would get a glimpse of your own blueprints one day. There is absolutely nothing like it. And that the richter scale that measures the joy inside of you?..

...that it would be blown straight through the roof.

- Winning the Super Bowl -

Which brings us to winning the Super Bowl. What does winning the Super Bowl look like in our stadiums? Feel like?

It happens when you are insanely in sync with your blueprint, insanely free of worry, stress or fear. Those things come at us on our opposing teams, as they do with all of us, but you are now more than equipped to handle them and holster them at your hip, rather than be drowned out or influenced by them.

It feels like you're sitting down for the first time, and nothing enters your head but relief, nothing taps your shoulder, nothing slides over and says, "but..." The second guessing, the shame, the inner-torture that you may not even be aware of now, will have come to a stand still. They will peek in, yes, and instead you will see them and you will put them back in their place - outside of you, not in you.

The goal? The touchdown? The win? Ecstasy in every moment. Joy in every moment. Compassion. Freedom in knowing how strong your boundaries are. Checked-in. You will feel the end of your skin pressing out, hairs tingling, knowing you are doing exactly what you were made to do, and absolutely nobody else, before or again. I kid you not. Grocery shopping becomes fun, a stop-over interesting and tired body more rested.

The goal is oxygen. Clean air. Knowledge. And knowing. And all the exhilaration, regeneration and hope that comes with it.

It's perfect.
Perfect.

And who else, really, would ever even consider saying that about this crazy thing called life?

I would. And you will. You can. Stick with me. If you can't see the goal posts now, the longer you hold my hand the closer we'll get to them and the more you will finally see them - through the thick of the trees you'll see the beam of bright light - through the thick of looming shadows that are the opposing team, I'll help you throw them off so those tall posts aren't just visible, but reachable too.

Joy. Compassion. Freedom. Curiosity. We are here.

Love,
Katherine

ACKNOWLEDGEMENTS

As you can imagine, I traveled a most interesting road to such a destination as this. My thanks and gratitude go to some of the best coaches ever: Bill Roth, Patti Roth, Dr. Ounanion, UCLA, Invia Betjoseph, Dr. Omaha, Bob and Linda Lemley, Lanse and Ginny Otis and Larry and Rhonda Sonnenburg.

To my Lord God and Savior, I love living my life with and around You. How could I have made the cut without You? And You were right, but I still wish I'd found You earlier. Thank you for showing me the road and for giving light to it in the night.

To my insane husband who sat next to me in the car for all of it. You held on and had fun somehow. Your grip is amazing. Let's do it again!

Thank you to those who have supported me, prayed for me and even cheered for me either here at home or from far, far away.

And finally, my dearest thanks to my fans around the globe, especially all those who have purchased, read and spread the word about my work. You've taught me so much and I am, as always, humbled and grateful. My love to you all.

RECOMMENDED RESOURCES

In alphabetical order:

Alcoholics Anonymous
(AA)

Codependents Anonymous
(CoDA)

Dr. John Omaha
Affect Centered Therapy
(ACT)
johnomahaenterprises.com

New Life Ministries
newlife.org
1-800-NEW-LIFE
(1-800-639-5433)
for therapists in your area and more

Plutchik's Wheel of Emotions

Sex and Love Addiction Anonymous
(SLAA)

Twelve Step Programs

RECOMMENDED READING

In alphabetical order:

12 "Christian" Beliefs that Can Drive You Crazy
Cloud and Townsend

Boundaries
Cloud and Townsend

Drama of the Gifted Child
Miller

Feeling Good
Burns

The Feeling Good Handbook
Burns

Nice Girls Don't Get the Corner Office
Frankel

Safe People
Cloud and Townsend

OTHER BOOKS BY THE AUTHOR

Telling the Truth
The Groundbreaking Articles That Saved West Coast Swing

Setting Dancers Free
The Weekly Notes That Rocked the World of West Coast Swing

ABOUT THE AUTHOR

Katherine Eastvold has more than twenty years of combined experience working with people at deep and intimate levels. She is heavily trained in both peer counseling and conflict resolution and did her graduate coursework at the nation's top graduate school of education. She has worked with a wide array of clientele atmospheres, from K-12 classrooms to nursing homes and from inner city street missions to corporate offices, helping others become empowered as well as free to expand their educations, perspectives and knowledge.

She is an author of two other books, *Telling the Truth* and *Setting Dancers Free*, both exposing corruption and scandal in the ballroom dance community where she met her husband Nick. They currently reside in Camarillo, CA and spend their free time exploring and adventuring both back roads and the wide seas.

www.ingramcontent.com/pod-product-compliance
Lightning Source LLC
Chambersburg PA
CBHW071858020426
42331CB00010B/2565